4

Ingredients

GLUTEN FREE

Ingredients
GLUTEN FREE

4 Ingredients
PO Box 400
Caloundra QLD 4551

ABN: 19 307 118 068

www.4ingredients.co.uk
info@4ingredients.co.uk

4 Ingredients Gluten Free

Cover & Formatting: Allure Creative, www.allurecreative.com.au
Printing & Binding: CPI Mackays, Chatham ME5 8TD

UK Publisher: Simon & Schuster (020) 7316 1900
AUS Distributor: Simon & Schuster +61 2 9983 6600
NZ Distributor: Random House +64 9 444 7197

ISBN: 978-0-85720-057-0

Foreword

Since we started our *4 Ingredients* journey only 2 years ago, we have done *over* 400 appearances and book signings and literally met thousands of fabulous people from all around Australia and New Zealand. At these events, one of the most common questions we were asked was 'Do you have any gluten free recipes?' and the answer is, in fact, 'YES', we have *hundreds* of absolutely gorgeous gluten free recipes!

We had dabbled with gluten free cooking (Rach's husband Paul has an intolerance to it) however it wasn't until we continued to receive this question so frequently that we considered doing a book dedicated to those who are completely intolerant of gluten.

As we started researching we were ASTOUNDED to see statistics showed that 1 in 100 will have coeliac disease. How many people are still undiagnosed? Surprisingly, what we also discovered was that there are a large number of people out there who just want to cut back on wheat, rye, oats and barley in their everyday diets, choosing to do so not because of intolerance to gluten but as a lifestyle choice.

Initially we thought finding recipes would be a MAMMOTH task when you consider that gluten is found in so many items. It's in some flavoured commercial spreads, sauces and flavoured chocolate, some hams, almost ALL of the biscuits stocked at supermarkets, some sausages, packet sauce and soup mixes, most cake mixes, common breads, tortillas, icing sugar and a whole lot more … compiling this book has been a huge learning curve and it's also been incredibly interesting to rise to the challenge of substituting normal flours for buckwheat, rice flour and other gluten free flours. But like all things, if you seek, you shall find; if you ask, you shall learn, and if you persist it will happen!

We would like to take this opportunity to thank our always supportive husbands, family and friends, as well as Graham, Cheryl and all the team at The Coeliac Society of Australia which has been an invaluable source of information and guidance while compiling this book.

4 Ingredients Gluten Free, with over 400 simple, speedy and scrumptious recipes, is proof that a gluten free lifestyle can be delicious!

Best wishes and happy cooking!

Kim & Rachael

WARNING!

In an effort to make this book as user-friendly as possible we chose to *list the ingredients* that we used in many of our recipes to help you when shopping.

These ingredients at time of writing were endorsed by The Australian Coeliac Society as being gluten free. And *many* of them clearly have 'gluten free' marked on them.

However, changes may happen. Manufacturing processes change, ingredients change, labels change.

As a precaution ALWAYS check the labels for updated information and warnings to ensure what you think you are eating is what you are actually eating!

What is Gluten?

> Gluten is a protein found in grains including wheat, rye, oats and barley.

Gluten is found in some soups, mayonnaises and many processed foods as well as in wheat starch binders and fillers. Gluten can also be found in medications and some vitamins.

People with coeliac disease are sensitive to gluten which damages the lining of the small bowel. This damage can lead to symptoms including fatigue, anaemia, irritable bowel type symptoms and vitamin and mineral deficiencies.

When choosing products it is very important to check the product's ingredient listing.

Under the Australian and New Zealand Food Standards Code, if an ingredient is derived from wheat, rye, barley or oats, then this must be declared. Therefore ingredients where the source grain is not identified are from a non-gluten containing grain and are gluten free.

Another FABULOUS source of information and help is your national or your state based Coeliac Society. On membership they send a pack loaded with information about the gluten free diet, an extremely helpful ingredient guide, a magazine and information on events such as shopping tours, information sessions and much more.

We highly recommend that any time you have a query you seek information from The Coeliac Society via the following websites or phone numbers:

Australia	www.coeliacsociety.com.au	1300 458 836
Ireland	www.coeliac.ie	01 872 1471
New Zealand	www.colourcards.com/coeliac	09 820 5157
United Kingdom	www.coeliac.org.uk	0845 305 2060

Gluten Foods

Did you know:

As written in the book *Gluten Free Baking* (with the Culinary Institute of America):

'Coeliac' is a Greek word referring to the abdomen and was first referenced by the Greek physician Araetaeus of Cappadocia, during the first or second century A.D. But it wasn't until after the Dutch famine of WWII, when wheat flour was scarce, that the connection between coeliac disease and the ingestion of wheat was made. A Dutch pediatrician Willem Karel Dicke made the connection in 1950!

Here is a helpful table supplied to us by the Australian Coeliac Society of foods that are good for a gluten free diet and foods that are not!

FOODS TO AVOID (CONTAIN GLUTEN)	FOODS TO INCLUDE (GLUTEN FREE)
Barley	Amaranth flour
Beer unless gluten free	Arrowroot
Cornflour from wheat	Baby rice cereal
Oatmeal	Besan or chickpea flour
Pearl barley	Buckwheat flour
Rye	Carob
Triticale	Coconut flour
Wheat bran	Gluten free flour mixes
Wheat flour: Plain, self raising, whole grain	Lentil flour
Wheat varieties: atta, bourghul, burgar, bulghur, bulgur, dinkel, durum, emmer, farina, graham, kumat, semolina, spelt	Lupin flour
	Maize: cornflour, cornmeal, polenta
	Millet
	Potato flour
	Quinoa
	Rice (all varieties including glutinous)
	Rice flour / rice bran
	Sago
	Sorghum
	Soy: flour, bean
	Tapioca
	Teff

In the Cupboard

As in *4 Ingredients 1* and *2* we have a suggested list of ingredients that you may want to stock to help you create wonderful meals and treats from the following pages. All the items on the following list can be found in Gluten Free stores, organic supermarkets and often in your local supermarkets. If you can't find an item in your store, don't be afraid to ask your supermarket manager to order it for you.

Please note: Again, in this book we have not included salt, pepper and water as part of the 4 ingredients.

SAVOURY	SWEET
Cold pressed extra virgin macadamia nut oil	Caster sugar
Extra virgin macadamia oil spray	Cinnamon
Free range eggs	Condensed milk
Fresh vegetables	Cream
Garlic	Cream cheese
Gluten free basil pesto	Dessicated coconut
Gluten free BBQ sauce	Evaporated milk
Gluten free beef & chicken stock	Food colouring
Gluten free bread crumbs	Fresh fruit
Gluten free curry powder	Gluten free plain & self raising flour
Gluten free Dijon mustard	Honey
Gluten free mayonnaise	Jams: apricot, strawberry
Gluten free soy sauce	Maize cornflour (100% gluten free)
Gluten free spaghetti & noodles	Marmalade
Gluten free stocks	Mixed fruit
Gluten free sweet chilli sauce	Mixed spices
Gluten free vegetable seasoning	Nutmeg
Gluten free Worcestershire sauce	Pkt bamboo skewers
Lemons	Sugar (raw, brown)
Minced ginger	Tin of pie apple
Peppercorns	Tinned fruit: pineapple, pear
Pine nuts	Vanilla essence
Rice	
Sea salt	
Sesame seeds	
Sour cream	
Tomato sauce	
Vinegar (not malt)	

Guide to Weights & Measures

A big fancy conversion table is not required,
as all you need to make the recipes within 4 Ingredients are:

1 teaspoon (1 tsp.)
1 tablespoon (1 tbs.)
1 cup (250ml)
or the following:

Product	Grams per Cup	Product	Grams per Cup
Almond Meal	170	Nuts–Pecans	120
BBQ Sauce	280	Nuts–Pine nuts	160
Butter	230	Nuts–Pistachios	120
Basil Pesto	260	Nuts–Walnuts	100
Breadcrumbs	130	Pasta (dried)	75
Brown sugar, packed	220	Pasta Sauce	175
Caster sugar	200	Peanut butter	260
Cheese	100	Popcorn	40
Chutney	300	Raisins	170
Cornflakes	120	Rice	185
Cornflour	120	Rice bubbles	80
Desiccated Coconut	120	Rolled oats	100
Dried apricots	160	Salsa	175
Dried mixed fruit	170	Self raising flour	175
Flour–Plain	175	Sour cream	320
Flour–Self Raising	175	Sultanas	170
Honey	320	Sugar–White	220
Icing Sugar	120	Sugar–Raw	200
Jam	320	Sweet chilli sauce	320
Maple Syrup	240	Tandoori paste	225
Mayonnaise	260	Tomato paste	260
Natural Muesli	110	Tomato Sauce	280
Nuts–Almonds	160	Yoghurt	250

Abbreviations Used

Gram	g
Kilogram	kg
Millilitre	ml
Litre	ltr

Oven Temperature Guide

Making friends with your oven really helps when cooking. Basically the Celsius temperature is about half the Fahrenheit temperature.

Most ovens these days offer the option to bake or fan bake (amongst others); as a rule, the fan-assisted option will greatly increase the temperature in your oven and will decrease cooking times.

Our recipes have been compiled assuming a fan-forced oven unless otherwise stated. If, however, your oven is conventional as a general rule of thumb fan-forced cooking temperatures are increased by 20°C (this may vary between models). So if the recipe reads 'bake for 1 hour at 200°C' that will be 1 hour at 220°C in a conventional oven.

Here's some help:

	Slow	Slow	Mod	Mod	Mod hot	Mod hot	Hot	Hot	Very hot
Fahrenheit	275	300	325	350	375	400	425	450	475
Celsius	140	150	165	180	190	200	220	230	240
Gas Mark	1	2	3	4	5	6	7	8	9

Healthy Food Substitutes

We are blessed with being different and special in our own right, and that also goes for the way our bodies operate. The one thing we all have in common is the essential requirement for *LOADS* of nutrients to keep our bodies functioning at their optimal levels.

A terrific way to satisfy the body's basic nutritional requirements is to eat more organic or home grown products which we use wherever possible. Not only are these full to the brim with a fabulous array of nutrients, but they are incredibly delicious.

However not everyone can readily access these products. We did not include these in our recipes, opting instead to add this section, which we feel is vital to you and your family's health.

For information regarding organic foods we recommend our good friend Cyndi O'Meara's book *Changing Habits Changing Lives*.

PRODUCT	SUBSTITUTE
White Sugar	• Brown sugar • Organic raw sugar*
Oil	• Avocado oil • Cold pressed extra virgin olive oil* • Cold pressed macadamia nut oil* • Grapeseed oil
Spray Oil	• Cold pressed macadamia nut oil *
Flours	• Gluten free plain flour * • Gluten free self raising flour * • Rice flour *
Margarine	• Butter*
Eggs	• Free range eggs*
Milk	• Organic milk* • Raw milk (pasteurised only milk)
Pasta	• Gluten free pasta*
Honey	• Manuka honey* • Organic honey*
Jams	• Homemade jams made from raw ingredients. • Organic jam*
Soy Sauce	• Gluten free soy sauce*

*Note — all ingredients with an asterisk * can now be bought in your local supermarket. Where possible buy products labeled 'certified organic' as these products have passed all the stringent tests to ensure that they really are organic and therefore are loaded with nutrients and flavour.*

Finally!

A cookbook to take the guess work out of gluten free cooking!

"Finally a *4 Ingredients* recipe book that is gluten free! This will save me a lot of time when cooking and shopping for my daughter, Molly, who has coeliac disease. This book will transform my life when it comes to meal planning and preparation. *4 Ingredients* will not only make my life easier but the recipes are so simple the kids can be involved too!"

Jenny Edwards

"As a busy, working mother of two it is hard to find time to make great gluten free recipes without compromising the nutrition of our families. With *4 Ingredients* I can now make tasty gluten free food, eat healthily and still have some 'me time'. Soccer nights will no longer need to be takeaway with your quick and easy recipes, saving me not only time but money. My husband will no longer have the excuse that cooking gluten free is difficult. Thank you *4 Ingredients!*"

Taryn Stephenson

"I was thrilled when I heard about your new book; finally I will be able to make gluten free meals for my friend who is a coeliac without the fear of accidentally giving her 'gluten poisoning'. Thanks *4 Ingredients!*"

Carol

"At last a gluten free cookbook that doesn't have dozens of ingredients! Thanks Kim and Rachael for revolutionizing the way we cook gluten free. I work full time and have two coeliacs in the family; myself and my daughter. As a dedicated 'cookbook junkie', I find I don't cook regularly from most of my cookbooks. Your new cookbook won't be relegated to the back of the cupboard; it will be used nightly to produce flavoursome and quick gluten free meals for all the family to enjoy."

Cathy Di Bella

Table of Contents

Breakfasts

All happiness depends on a leisurely breakfast.

John Gunther

Almond Pancakes

MAKES 12

- *3 free range eggs*
- *1 cup (170g) almond meal*
- *½ cup (125g) Greek yoghurt*
- *2 tbs. (30g) butter for frying*

Break the eggs into a bowl and whisk. Add the almond meal and enough yoghurt to form a batter. Heat the butter in a small non-stick frying pan over medium/hot heat and when melted pour in a little of the pancake batter. Cook for a minute or two until it begins to set. Flip the pancake over to cook the other side.

Optional: Delicious served with a dollop of yoghurt and a sprinkle of brown sugar.

Apple Fritters

- *1 slice GF bread, grated*
- *1 tsp. cinnamon sugar*
- *1 free range egg*
- *1 medium apple, grated*

Combine first 3 ingredients with 1 tbs. water and mix well. Add apple and combine. Drop by tbs. into a hot non-stick frying pan. Cook until underside is golden, flip gently and cook other side until golden brown.

Basic Crepes

MAKES 35

- 3 free range eggs
- 1½ cups (375ml) milk
- 2¼ cups (380g) GF plain flour
- 1 tbs. olive oil

Blend the first 3 ingredients together with 1½ cups (375ml) of water using an electric beater. Heat a non-stick frying pan and add the oil, swirling it around to coat the entire surface. Poor enough mixture to coat the base of the pan and swirl in a circular motion so the batter is even. Cook for about 2 minutes or until the bottom is light brown and flip over to cook the other side.

Optional: Serve with Toffee Bananas (see Breakfasts).

Note: This batter will keep for a couple of days refrigerated.

Bircher Muesli

SERVES 1

- ½ cup (55g) natural GF muesli
- ¼ cup (60ml) orange juice
- 2 tbs. natural yoghurt
- 1 green apple, grated

Soak the muesli in the juice for 15 minutes. Mix in remaining ingredients and serve!

Baked Raspberry French Toast

SERVES 6

A deliciously different way to prepare French toast.

- ¾ cup (240g) raspberry jam
- 12 slices GF bread, crusts removed
- 6 free range eggs
- 1 cup (250ml) milk

Preheat oven to 200°C. Spread jam on 1 side of 6 slices of gluten free bread and cover with remaining bread to form 6 sandwiches. Beat eggs and milk until frothy. Pour just enough egg mixture into well greased pan to cover bottom of a baking dish. Arrange sandwiches in pan. Pour remaining egg mixture over top. Bake in oven for about 20 minutes or until golden and set.

Optional: Yummy drizzled with pure maple syrup.

Buckwheat Pancakes

SERVES 2

Recipe by Melissa Perran.

- 1 cup (170g) buckwheat flour
- 1 free range egg
- 2 tsb. (30g) butter
- 2 tbs. pure maple syrup

Mix all ingredients together in a bowl with 1 cup (250ml) of water (use more water if mixture is too thick). In a non-stick frying pan over medium heat, dollop mixture into it. Cook for 1 minute and flip it over and cook for another minute.

Optional: Top with fresh fruit jam or cream. Substitute buckwheat flour for GF self raising flour.

Cheese Omelette

MAKES 2

- 3 free range eggs, separated
- ½ cup (50g) grated cheese
- 1 tbs. (15g) butter

Beat egg whites until stiff. Lightly fold in beaten yolks and 3 tbs. (45ml) cold water, cheese and a pinch of sea salt. Melt butter in a non-stick frying pan and when hot pour in mixture. Cook till golden underneath. Turn with an egg flipper.

Note: Water gives the omelette a fluffy texture.

Citrus Pancakes

MAKES 4

- 1 cup (175g) GF self raising flour
- 1 free range egg
- 1 cup (250ml) milk
- 2 mandarins, grate the zest and cut the segments

Combine flour, egg and a pinch of sea salt. Beat gradually, adding milk until thick and smooth. Add mandarin zest and segments. Heat non-stick frying pan. Pour desired quantity into frying pan, cook until bubbling on top and then flip.

Optional: Serve with pure maple syrup, lemon juice and sugar, honey or stewed fruits.

Tip: Another tasty topping is the citrus-infused maple syrup. Add some orange peel to a bowl of pure maple syrup and allow to sit for an hour before using.

Damper

SERVES 6

- 4 cups (680g) GF self raising flour
- 4 tsp. GF baking powder
- 2 cups (500ml) milk
- 2 tbs. golden syrup

Preheat oven to 180°C. Together with a tsp. of sea salt, combine all ingredients (if a little wet, add extra flour). Shape into a high, round bun and on a paper lined baking tray bake for 30 minutes.

Optional: Serve warm with lashings of butter and golden syrup.

Feta & Leek Omelette

SERVES 2

- 1 tbs. (15g) butter
- 1 leek, washed and thinly sliced
- 4 free range eggs, beaten
- 100g feta, crumbled

Heat butter in a non-stick frying pan, toss in leek and stir fry for 3–4 minutes or until soft, taking care not to burn. Pour in eggs and season with sea salt and pepper, cook over medium heat for 5 minutes or until the eggs are no longer runny. Sprinkle with feta, fold in half, allow feta to warm before cutting into wedges and serving.

Grilled Apple, Banana & Ricotta Stack

MAKES 1

This is a charming breakfast — your guests will be impressed!

- *1 apple*
- *1 banana*
- *2 tbs. reduced fat fresh ricotta*
- *1 tbs. honey*

Slice and grill the apple for 3 minutes. Layer apple and banana. Top with ricotta and drizzle honey over all.

Optional: This is also delicious done with pear rather than apple, or a combination of both.

Ham and Egg Quiche

MAKES 6

From Sharyn Seligmann ... *Faaabalish!*

- *6 round slices of GF ham*
- *6 free range eggs*
- *1 cup (100g) grated cheese*
- *2 tbs. chopped parsley*

Preheat oven to 180°C. Line 6 large non-stick muffin cases with ham. Beat eggs, season with sea salt and pepper and pour into ham lined muffin cases. Top with cheese and parsley. Bake for 20 minutes or until set.

Optional: Instead of parsley these could be topped with tomato or pepper.

Lemon Butter

A recipe by Liz Woodcraft.

- ½ cup (115g) butter
- 1½ cups (330g) sugar
- 6 free range eggs
- 3 large lemons

Melt butter and sugar in the microwave. In a separate bowl, beat eggs until frothy. Grate the lemon rind of 1 lemon finely, then juice the 3 lemons. Add that and the eggs to the butter and cook on med/high in the microwave for 5 minutes stirring every minute.

Muesli Smoothie

SERVES 1–2

A recipe from the lovely Kim Morrison.

- 1 cup (250ml) milk or GF soy milk
- 1 frozen banana
- ½ cup (55g) GF toasted muesli
- 3 tbs. fruit yoghurt

Place all ingredients in blender and process until smooth.

Optional: Add ice if you would like it colder.

Quick Muffins

MAKES 6

- 1¾ cup (300g) GF self raising flour
- 4 tbs. GF mayonnaise
- 1 cup (250ml) milk
- 4 rashers of rindless bacon, diced and fried

Preheat oven to 180°C. Mix all ingredients until just combined. Fill muffin cups two-thirds full. Bake for about 20–25 minutes.

Optional: Substitute bacon for whatever you like, ham, chives, semi-dried tomatoes, feta cheese, as long as it is gluten free.

Raspberry Delights

SERVES 4

- 1 punnet fresh raspberries
- 400g tub Greek yoghurt
- 1 tbs. finely grated lemon zest

Puree raspberries until just smooth. Combine yoghurt and lemon rind. Gently mix together in a slow swirling fashion. Spoon into four serving glasses and refrigerate for 15 minutes before serving.

Optional: Drizzle with honey to serve.

Sweet Breakfast Toast

MAKES 1

Recipe by Cyndi O'Meara.

- 1 slice GF bread
- 1 tsp. peanut butter
- 1 tsp. honey
- 1 small banana, mashed

Toast the GF bread, spread peanut butter, honey and banana in layers onto the toast.

Optional: Sprinkle with pine nuts.

Toffee Bananas

MAKES 4

- 2 tbs. (30g) butter
- ½ cup (110g) brown sugar
- 3–4 bananas, sliced

Add butter to a non-stick frying pan on medium heat. Add sugar and stir until dissolved, add banana slices and cook until warmed through.

Optional: Serve wrapped in GF crepes ... Yummmmmmmmmmm!

Tru-Blu Eggs

MAKES 4

- *4 free range eggs*
- *12 asparagus spears (cleaned)*
- *220g blue brie cheese*
- *¼ cup (60ml) garlic oil*

Add asparagus to salted, boiling water and cook for 2 minutes or until tender. Remove and set aside. Fill a large saucepan ¾ with water and bring to boil. Stir clockwise rapidly, gently crack the eggs into swirling water one after the other (the moving water helps the eggs roll and form separate balls). Reduce to a light simmer. Poach until yolks are medium (1–2 minutes, or 3 minutes for firm yolk or extra large egg). With a slotted spoon carefully lift and drain eggs from the pan. Place 3 asparagus spears on a plate, pop an egg on top of the asparagus and the softened blue cheese on top of egg, drizzle with garlic oil.

Tip: To make your own garlic oil, fill a sealable jar with extra virgin olive oil and 3 cloves of split garlic. Sit overnight for flavour to infuse before using.

Dips

Artichoke Dip

- ⅔ cup (160ml) olive oil
- 100g jar artichokes, drained
- ⅔ cup (75g) grated parmesan cheese
- 1 clove garlic

Place all ingredients into a blender and process until nice and smooth. Season to taste.

Optional: Serve with a platter of fresh vegetable sticks; pepper, radish, carrot, celery etc.

Avo & Corn Dip

SERVES 6

Recipe from Jules Boag.

- 3 ripe avocados
- 2 tbs. sour cream
- ¼ cup GF creamed corn
- ¼ tsp. cayenne pepper

Mash and mix all ingredients together and serve with vegie sticks.

Basil Dip

Recipe by Laurent Vancam.

- *1 large bunch of fresh basil*
- *2 garlic cloves, crushed*
- *100g parmesan cheese, grated*
- *¼ cup (60ml) olive oil*

Blend all ingredients together and serve. Easy and ultra tasty!

Butter Bean & Mustard Topper

- *400g can butter beans, rinsed and drained*
- *1 tsp. GF whole grain or GF Dijon mustard*
- *3 tbs. (45ml) olive oil*
- *2 tbs. finely chopped fresh flat leafed parsley*

Place the beans and mustard into a blender, turn on and add the olive oil. You will probably need to add a little water to get to the desired consistency. Blend until smooth. Add the parsley and black pepper. Serve on GF crackers.

Note: Parsley is the world's most popular herb. It contains three times as much Vitamin C as oranges, twice as much iron as spinach, is rich in Vitamin A and contains folate, potassium and calcium.

Cinnamon Dip

MAKES 1 CUP

- *250g sour cream*
- *3 generous tsp. GF ground cinnamon*
- *1 tbs. brown sugar*

Place all ingredients into a bowl and mix well. Chill for at least 2 hours prior to serving to allow flavours time to develop. Serve with a platter of fresh fruit and dried apricots for dipping.

Corn Relish & Bacon Dip

MAKES 2 CUPS

This is D.E.L.I.S.H!

- *5 rindless bacon rashers, chopped*
- *250g jar GF corn relish*
- *300g sour cream*
- *¼ cup chopped spring onions*

Cook bacon in a non-stick frying pan on medium heat until nice and crispy (pat excess fat from rashers with absorbent paper). Place in a bowl and allow to cool. Add remaining ingredients and mix well. Refrigerate for 30 minutes before serving with your favourite GF crackers.

Dipping Chips

SERVES 4–6

These are divine!

- 4 GF tortillas
- 2 tbs. olive oil
- 1 tbs. fresh rosemary leaves, finely chopped
- 1 tsp. sea salt

Preheat oven to 180°C. Brush tortillas with oil and sprinkle with rosemary and sea salt. Place on a baking tray and bake in oven for 5–7 minutes or until browned on the edges and crisp. Cut into wedges to serve with dips.

Feta Dip

MAKES 1 CUP AND IS REALLY, REALLY TASTY.

- 200g feta
- ¼ cup (60ml) olive oil
- 1 garlic clove, crushed
- ¼ cup (60ml) milk

Place feta, oil and garlic into a food processor and blend until combined. While still processing, gently add milk in a slow stream and mix until a smooth paste forms. Chill before serving.

Optional: Serve with fresh vegie sticks or your favourite GF crackers.

Garlic Crisps

SERVES 4

These are a lighter option for use as a side dish or as dippers.

- *2 GF tortillas*
- *2 tbs.(30g) butter*
- *2 tbs. crushed garlic*

Preheat oven to 180°C. Mix butter with garlic and spread liberally over each tortilla. Cut into pie or wedge sized slices and place on a paper lined baking tray. Bake for 10 minutes or until lightly crispy.

Grilled Cheese Salsa Dip

A Mexicana marvel ... Too easy and too tasty!

- *250g edam or gouda cheese*
- *2 tbs. cream*
- *½ cup (85g) chunky tomato salsa*

Grate cheese and place in a small saucepan. Cook on low-medium stovetop, let cheese melt then add cream, stirring frequently to make sure cheese doesn't scorch the dish. Transfer to a warm dish, top with salsa.

Optional: Serve with fresh raw vegetable sticks and GF corn chips ... Mmmmmm!

Guacamole

SERVES 4

- *1 ripe avocado, mashed*
- *1 small ripe tomato, finely chopped*
- *½ a bunch coriander, chopped*
- *1 tbs. lime juice*

Place all ingredients in a bowl, season with sea salt and pepper, and mix. Chill before serving with GF corn chips.

Optional: Add a little finely chopped Spanish onion if desired.

Hint: Prepare ahead of time and place the avocado seed back into the dip to help prevent discolouration.

Hummus

MAKES ½ A CUP

- *300g can chickpeas*
- *1 garlic clove, crushed*
- *2 tbs. lemon juice*
- *1 tbs. tahini*

Blend all ingredients in a food processor.

Optional: Serve with julienne vegetables and GF crackers.

Oyster Dip

MAKES 1 CUP

- *100g tin smoked oysters, drained*
- *125g sour cream*

Using a fork, mash oysters in a bowl. Add ½ the sour cream and mix until combined (add more sour cream if needed). Chill before serving.

Roasted Aubergine Dip

MAKES 1 CUP

- *2 large aubergines, peeled and sliced*
- *1 lemon, juiced*
- *1 garlic clove, crushed*
- *2 tbs. tahini*

Preheat oven 180°C. Place aubergines on paper lined baking tray and cook for 30 minutes. When cooled, peel skin and discard. Place filling in a bowl with remaining ingredients and blend.

Tapenade

MAKES ½ A CUP

- ⅔ cup kalamata olives
- 1 clove garlic, crushed
- 2 tbs. fresh basil torn into small pieces
- 1½ tbs. olive oil

Place ingredients in a blender and process until smooth. Cover, chill and when needed serve with fresh vegie sticks or GF crackers.

Warm Cheese Dip

MAKES 2 CUPS

This is R.e.a.l.l.y Y.u.m.m.y!!

- 2 tbs. (30g) butter
- 250g sour cream
- 2 cups (200g) grated cheddar cheese
- ½ tsp. ground cumin

Melt butter in saucepan and add cumin stir over a low heat for a minute. Add sour cream and when warm, add cheddar cheese. Stir constantly until the cheese melts and the mixture is smooth. Serve warm with GF crackers and fresh vegie sticks.

Salad Dressings

You miss 100% of the shots you never take.

Wayne Gretzky

Blue Cheese Dressing

MAKES 1 CUP

- *30g blue cheese*
- *⅓ cup (85g) GF mayonnaise*
- *⅓ cup (80g) natural yoghurt*
- *3 tbs. freshly chopped chives*

Use a fork to mash the cheese in a small bowl. Add remaining ingredients and mix well. Season to taste with black pepper.

Balsamic Vinaigrette

MAKES 1 CUP

- *¼ cup (60ml) balsamic vinegar*
- *1 tbs. GF mustard*
- *¾ cup (185ml) extra virgin olive oil*

In a medium bowl, whisk together the vinegar and mustard. Slowly pour in the olive oil, whisking constantly until combined. Season with sea salt and pepper.

Note: Vinaigrette will keep in an airtight container in the fridge for up to one week. Whisk to combine just before serving.

Caramelised Balsamic Vinegar

MAKES 1 CUP

- ⅔ cup (165ml) balsamic vinegar
- ½ cup (110g) brown sugar

Bring ingredients to the boil slowly. Stir until sugar dissolves. Boil for 1 minute or until slightly thick. Allow to cool and store in refrigerator.

Classic Salad Dressing

MAKES ½ CUP

- 2 tbs. fresh lemon juice
- ¼ cup (60ml) extra virgin olive oil
- 1 tsp. GF Dijon mustard
- ½ clove garlic, crushed

Place all in a screw-top jar, season to taste and shake well.

Hint: When a jar of mustard is nearly empty, add some olive oil and wine vinegar and shake well for a delicious salad dressing.

Greek Yoghurt & Whole Egg Mayonnaise

This is absolutely SENSATIONAL and will make a salad eater of anyone!

- ⅔ part natural Greek yoghurt
- ⅓ part GF whole egg mayonnaise

Mix well and serve over salad.

Orange & Mustard Dressing

MAKES 2 CUPS

- ¾ cup (185ml) orange juice
- ⅓ cup (80g) GF wholegrain mustard
- 1 cup (250ml) walnut oil

Whisk all ingredients together, season with sea salt and pepper and then enjoy!

Peps Dressing

MAKES ¼ CUP

Recipe by Lea Van Dijk.

- 3 tbs. (45ml) extra virgin olive oil
- 2 tbs. (30ml) white wine vinegar
- 1 tsp. GF wholegrain mustard
- Ground pepper

Mix all ingredients together in a jar and shake well. Use straight away.

Salad Dressing

MAKES ⅓ CUP

- 2 tbs. (30ml) lemon juice
- ¼ cup (60ml) olive oil

Combine lemon juice and oil and mix well. Season with sea salt and pepper.

Thai Dressing

MAKES ⅓ CUP

- 2 tbs. sugar
- 2 tbs. lime juice
- ⅓ cup (80ml) fish sauce
- GF chilli powder to taste

Combine all ingredients in a screw-top jar and shake well.

Vinaigrette

MAKES 1 CUP

- ½ cup (125ml) olive oil
- ½ cup (125ml) white wine vinegar
- 4–6 sprigs flat-leaf parsley, finely chopped
- 2 tsp. GF Dijon mustard

Combine all ingredients in a screw-top jar and shake well.

Wasabi Dressing

MAKES ⅔ CUP

- 2 tsp. GF wasabi paste
- ⅓ cup (80ml) lemon juice
- ⅓ cup (80ml) peanut oil
- 2 tsp. finely chopped fresh coriander

Combine all ingredients in a screw-top jar and shake well.

Sauces

Inspiration follows aspiration.

Rabindranath Tagore

Basil Pesto

MAKES ½ CUP

- *½ cup (50g) pine nuts*
- *100g parmesan cheese, grated*
- *1 large bunch of fresh basil*
- *1 tbs. (15ml) olive oil*

Brown half of the pine nuts in a dry pan. Put first 3 ingredients into a blender and blitz. Mix with the olive oil.

Optional: Alter the flavour by adding a drop or two of lemon juice and one clove of garlic.

Caramel Sauce

MAKES 2 CUPS

This is heaven served over just about anything!

- *250ml double cream*
- *¾ cup (165g) brown sugar*
- *125g unsalted butter*

Combine all ingredients in a small saucepan and bring to the boil over medium heat. Simmer for 2 minutes.

Cranberry Compote

MAKES 1 CUP

- *1 brown onion, chopped*
- *½ cup cranberries*
- *2 tbs. brown sugar*
- *⅓ cup (80ml) balsamic vinegar*

Sauté onions with 2 tbs. water until clear, add cranberries, sugar and balsamic vinegar. Reduce heat and allow to simmer until caramelised.

Optional: Serve with turkey, chicken or even a dipping sauce to accompany a cheese platter.

Date, Pistachio, Orange & Mint Salsa

SERVES 4

A recipe from the lovely Marie McColl.

- *100g fresh dates, pitted and chopped*
- *2 tbs. pistachio kernels, chopped*
- *4 fresh mint stems, chopped*
- *2 oranges, peeled and cubed*

Mix all ingredients together to make a delicious salsa to serve with grilled lamb or pork or omit the dates and serve it atop a piece of your favourite grilled fish.

Easy Mocha Sauce

MAKES 2 CUPS

- *200g dark chocolate*
- *300ml double cream*
- *2 tsp. instant coffee*

Combine all ingredients and cook in microwave for 2 minutes, stopping to stir every 30 seconds.

Optional: Serve this with poached pears — simply stunning!

Garlic Butter

MAKES ⅓ CUP

- *¼ cup (60g) soft butter*
- *1 clove garlic, crushed*
- *1 tsp. lemon juice*
- *1 tsp. finely chopped parsley*

Mix all together and season with sea salt and pepper.

Garlic Cream Sauce

MAKES ⅓ CUP

- *1 tsp. extra virgin olive oil*
- *1 clove garlic, crushed*
- *1½ tbs. GF Worcestershire sauce*
- *⅓ cup (80ml) double cream*

Heat oil in a non-stick frying pan and add garlic. Lightly sauté and add Worcestershire sauce and cream stirring to combine. Heat through and dollop onto the top of your favourite steak.

Green Peppercorn Sauce

ENOUGH FOR 1

- *1½ tsp. green peppercorns*
- *¼ cup (60ml) double cream*

Add peppercorns to hot frying pan (if accompanying meat, add to the frying pan after cooking the meat and prior to washing). Reduce heat to medium. Cook stirring for 1 minute. Stir in cream. Simmer for 2 minutes or until sauce thickens. Delicious over steak served with baked potato and fresh vegetables.

Hollandaise Sauce

MAKES 1 CUP

- *3 free range egg yolks*
- *125g butter, melted*
- *2 tbs. (30ml) vinegar*

Place egg yolks in a mixing bowl and using an electric beater, beat eggs until pale and thick (about 10 minutes). Gradually add melted butter, continuously beating. Add vinegar last and season to taste.

Optional: Add tarragon for Bernaise sauce.

Hot Fudge Sauce

MAKES 1 CUP

You'll wish it made more!

- *200g chocolate, chopped*
- *1 cup GF marshmallows, chopped*
- *1 cup (250ml) cream*

Combine all ingredients in a microwave dish and heat on high, stirring every 30 seconds until nice and smooth.

Optional: Serve drizzled over the peanut butter ice cream pie (see Desserts) ... Oooh La La!

Lemon Aioli

MAKES ½ CUP

- *½ cup (130g) GF mayonnaise*
- *1 clove garlic, crushed*
- *2 tbs. lemon juice (and a little lemon zest if desired)*

Mix ingredients together, season with sea salt and pepper and chill for several hours before serving, allowing time for flavours to infuse. Works well with almost any fish dish!

Mayonnaise

MAKES 1½ CUPS

- 1 large free range egg
- 2 tsp. white wine vinegar
- ½ tsp. sea salt
- 1¼ cup (300ml) sunflower oil

Put the egg, vinegar and sea salt into a food processor and turn on. Slowly pour in the oil. The longer you leave the machine on the thicker the mayonnaise will get.

Optional: Add a tsp. of GF Dijon mustard.

Mint Glaze

- 1 tbs. finely chopped mint
- 1 tbs. lemon juice
- 1 tbs. sugar

Place all ingredients plus 1 tbs. boiling water into a small saucepan and cook over a low heat for 5 minutes. Allow to stand for 30 minutes and serve glazed over roast lamb.

Mushroom Sauce

MAKES 2 CUPS

Rach's number 1 favourite!!

- *⅓ cup (50g) butter*
- *2 cups of mushrooms, sliced*
- *1 GF beef stock cube mixed with ½ cup (125ml) of hot water*
- *¾ cup (185ml) double cream*

Melt butter in a non-stick frying pan and add mushrooms, cooking for about 3–5 minutes or until soft. Add beef stock and cream and simmer until sauce thickens slightly. Serve with your favourite steak or some grilled chicken.

Quick Fire Chutney

MAKES APPROX. 2 CUPS

Recipe by Chef Dan Primmer.

- *½ red onion, chopped into chunks*
- *2 pears, chopped into chunks*
- *2 tbs. brown sugar*
- *½ tbs. chopped mint*

In a hot non-stick frying pan, sauté onions with a little water for 2 minutes. Add pears and continue to sauté until onions are clear and pears soften. Add ¼ cup water and sugar, reduce heat to low and simmer until liquid reduces. Remove from heat and allow to cool before gently stirring through the mint.

Note: This is sensational served over grilled chicken or pork and a great way to use those over ripe pears!

Raita

MAKES 2 CUPS

- 1 cup (250g) natural yoghurt
- 1 small cucumber, chopped finely
- 1 tbs. chopped fresh mint
- 1 small vine-ripened tomato, diced

Mix all ingredients together and season well.

Raspberry Sauce

MAKES ½ CUP

- 125g fresh raspberries
- 2 tbs. GF icing sugar
- 2 tsp. orange juice

Blend ingredients until smooth. Delicious drizzled over ice cream or swirled through cheesecakes (see Desserts, Cheesecake Filling).

Note: Strain to remove seeds.

Salsa

MAKES 1 CUP

- 1 avocado, diced
- 1 tsp. finely chopped red chilli
- Juice of ½ lime
- ¼ of one red pepper, diced

Combine altogether and serve over grilled pork … *YUM!*

Satay Sauce

MAKES 3 CUPS

Recipe by Chef Dan Primmer.

- *1 onion, diced*
- *1 cup (260g) crunchy peanut butter*
- *2 cups (500ml) coconut cream*
- *4 stems fresh chopped coriander*

In a non-stick frying pan sauté onions in a little water until translucent. Add peanut butter and coconut cream, over low heat stir until combined. When warmed through, add coriander, stir and serve.

Optional: This is delicious over kebabs and dolloped on top of Sweet Potato Cakes (see Potatoes).

Tartare Sauce

MAKES ¾ CUP

Recipe by Brett McCosker.

- *½ cup (125g) natural yoghurt*
- *1 tbs. drained capers, chopped*
- *2 gherkins, finely chopped*
- *1 tbs. finely chopped flat-leaf parsley*

Mix ingredients together and chill, allowing time for flavours to infuse prior to serving.

Tempura Batter

MAKES APPROX. 2 CUPS

- 1¼ cup (150g) maize cornflour
- 280ml soda water (real cold)

Sift flour in a bowl and add a pinch of sea salt. Make a well in the centre and add soda water, mix well until smooth and lump free. Set aside for 10–15 minutes before using.

Optional: Use small cut vegetables and meats and shallow fry.

White Sauce

MAKES 1 CUP

- 2 tbs. (30g) butter
- 2 tbs. GF plain flour
- 1 cup (250ml) milk

Melt butter in saucepan and remove from heat. Stir in flour and blend in milk. Return to heat, stir until sauce boils and thickens, and simmer for 2 minutes. Season with sea salt and pepper and add extra milk if required.

Tip: This is delicious flavoured with orange zest and freshly chopped parsley served over corned beef.

Cocktail Food

From small beginnings come great things.

Proverb

Asparagus Wraps

SERVES 6

- *2 bunches asparagus, ends trimmed*
- *8 slices prosciutto, cut into long, 1 cm wide strips*
- *2 tbs. (30ml) extra virgin olive oil*
- *2 tbs. (30ml) balsamic vinegar*

Preheat oven 180°C. Wrap a strip of prosciutto around each spear, creating a long, spiral effect. Place each spear on a baking tray, drizzle with oil and season with sea salt and pepper. Bake for 5–6 minutes. Pop onto plate and serve trickled with balsamic vinegar.

Baked Haloumi

SERVES 4

- *250g pkt haloumi cheese, drained and cut into 3 cm cubes*
- *2 tbs. GF plain flour*
- *3 tbs. (45ml) olive oil*
- *2 tbs. (30ml) fresh lemon juice*

Place GF flour on small plate, season with sea salt and pepper and evenly coat haloumi. Heat oil in non-stick frying pan over high heat, add haloumi and turn occasionally for 2 minutes or until golden brown. Transfer to serving plate, sprinkle with lemon juice and season with pepper.

Caramelised Macadamia Camembert

SERVES 4

Try this!

- *125g quality camembert cheese*
- *⅓ cup roasted macadamia nuts*
- *1 cup (220g) white sugar*

Place camembert wheel onto a heat-resistant plate or platter. Put sugar in a heavy-based pan. Cook on a low heat, without stirring, for 1–2 minutes or until sugar has melted and is dark golden brown. The pan may need to be tilted to ensure sugar melts evenly. Add chopped macadamia nuts and stir to coat. Remove from heat and stand on a wooden board until bubbles subside. Pour caramel and nuts over cheese. Stand for a couple of hours until set. The caramel will soften and seep into the cheese, giving a bittersweet flavour. Serve with your favourite GF crackers.

Chicken & Chorizo Skewers

MAKES 16

- *1 chicken breast, cubed*
- *1 GF chorizo sausage, sliced into same size as chicken cubes*
- *Extra virgin olive oil spray*
- *½ cup (85g) salsa*

Thread meats onto a skewer (or toothpick for a bite sized serving). Spray lightly before grilling. Serve warm with salsa as a dipping sauce.

Date and Walnut Pears

SERVES 4

- 1 large ripe pear
- 1 tbs. cream cheese
- 2 dried dates, finely chopped
- 1½ tbs. finely chopped walnuts

Cut pear into quarters and remove the core. Combine remaining ingredients together and top evenly over the pieces of pear. Serve.

Fried Calamari

SERVES 4–6

These are quick, easy and ALWAYS a hit!

- 3 cups (525g) GF plain flour
- 4 tbs. of mixed dried herb seasoning
- 4 fillets of whole fresh squid, cleaned, cut into 2 cm thick rings or strips
- 2 cups (500ml) sunflower oil

In a bowl, combine flour with dried herbs and add the squid. Toss until the squid is coated with the mixture, then gently shake off excess flour and drop a few pieces at a time into in a saucepan of hot oil. Take care not to add too many so they don't stick together. Fry for 1–2 minutes and remove immediately and place onto absorbent paper. Repeat till all the squid is cooked and serve warm.

Optional: Delicious served with Lemon Aioli (see Sauces).

Fried Chorizo with Garlic

SERVES 6

- *4 GF chorizo sausages*
- *2 cloves garlic, finely chopped*
- *4 stems flat leaf parsley, chopped*

Cut sausages in slices and cook in a large heated frying pan, stirring until crisp. Drain on absorbent paper. Return sausage slices to the pan together with the garlic and heat through, just before serving toss in the parsley.

Optional: Serve warm on toothpicks.

Marinated & Baked Olives

SERVES 6

- *500g green olives, pitted*
- *1 lemon, peel only*
- *2 sprigs rosemary, leaves only*
- *2 cloves garlic, thinly sliced*

Preheat oven to 200°C. Place olives in a baking dish and, with a rolling pin, gently push down so skin splits. Mix in the lemon peel, rosemary and garlic. Cook for 15 minutes and serve while warm.

Optional: Add 1 tbs. olive oil to the mix.

Minted Lamb Balls

SERVES 4

A recipe from Janelle McCosker.

- *500g minced lamb*
- *2 tsp. GF curry powder*
- *6–8 stems mint, chopped*

Mix all ingredients together and roll into bite sized balls and fry in a non-stick frying pan until crunchy on the outside (this means it is cooked well on the inside).

Optional: These are lovely served with Raita as a dipping sauce.

Parmesan Crisps

MAKES 6

A recipe by Lorraine Leeson ... *D.I.V.I.N.E!!!!*

- *200g wedge parmesan cheese*
- *1 tbs. sesame seeds*

Preheat oven to 200°C. Line a tray with baking paper and place 6 egg rings on top. Into each, thinly grate enough parmesan to cover the base. Top with a sprinkle of sesame seeds, gently remove egg rings and bake for 5–6 minutes or until the cheese melts into lacey discs. Allow to cool and serve as a nibble with drinks or as an accompaniment to your meal.

Optional: Substitute sesame seeds with a sprinkle of smokey paprika or a smattering of your favourite fresh herb.

Pear & Roquefort Bites

MAKES 16

- *2 fresh ripe pears, peeled and cubed*
- *125g Roquefort cheese, cubed*

Thread one cube of each onto a toothpick and serve immediately.

Ricotta & Prosciutto Baked Pies

MAKES 12

A recipe from the vibrant Perditta O'Connor.

- *5 slices prosciutto*
- *400g fresh ricotta*
- *6 sprigs fresh thyme, leaves picked*
- *1 bunch chives, coarsely chopped*

Preheat oven 180°C. Line the base and sides of each mini-muffin pan with prosciutto. Combine ricotta, thyme and chives in a bowl. Distribute mixture evenly into each muffin section and bake for 15 minutes or until set. Remove tray and set aside for another 15 minutes to cool before serving.

Optional: Season ricotta, thyme and chives with sea salt and pepper. Bake topped with some halved cherry tomatoes.

Salmon Paté

MAKES 1 CUP

- 210g can pink salmon, drained and bones removed
- 60g cream cheese, softened
- 1 tbs. GF mayonnaise
- 1–2 tbs. lemon juice

In a processor place the salmon. Add remaining ingredients, season with sea salt and pepper and blend until smooth. Serve with your favourite GF crackers.

Spinach and Cashew Paté

MAKES 1 CUP

- 120g cashew nuts
- 2 x 100g bags spinach leaves
- ½ tsp. grated nutmeg

Steam the spinach just enough till it's wilted. Blitz the cashews in a blender until finely ground and then add the spinach and nutmeg. Blitz to combine.

Optional: For a flavour variation add a generous tbs. of blue cheese.

Strawberry Sweet & Sour

SERVES 4

A recipe from Lorraine Leeson ... This will make an impact — TRY IT!!

- *300g strawberries, washed*
- *¼ cup (55g) brown sugar*
- *½ cup (160g) sour cream*

Place brown sugar and sour cream in separate ramekins, dip a strawberry into sour cream and then into the sugar ... Savour the flavour!

Hint: Always wash strawberries before you remove their stalks, otherwise water will get into the fruit and spoil their flavour.

Optional: Rach and Kim have a fourth ingredient with this one — a glass of bubbles — enjoy!

Tangy Cheese Balls

MAKES 24

- *125g cream cheese, softened*
- *30g blue cheese, finely crumbled*
- *2 tbs. orange zest*
- *50g mixed nuts, finely chopped*

Combine cream cheese, blue cheese and orange zest. Form into small balls and roll in nuts. Chill for an hour, or until firm, and serve.

Teriyaki Scallops

SERVES 4

A recipe from the talented Dan Primmer, chef extraordinaire!

- 18 scallops
- ½ cup GF teriyaki sauce
- 2 tbs. diced pickled ginger
- 1 tbs. toasted sesame seeds

Marinate scallops in teriyaki sauce for 1 hour. Pour into frying pan and cook over medium heat for 5 minutes, flipping scallops half way. Serve as an appetiser on Chinese spoons, garnished with ginger and sprinkled with sesame seeds.

Wheel of Brie

SERVES 4

This is sensational.

- 125g wheel of brie
- 1 tbs. GF basil pesto
- 30g marinated roasted red peppers, sliced
- 2 tbs. pine nuts

Preheat oven to 150°C. On a baking paper lined tray, gently cut the top off the brie wheel. Smear with pesto, top with peppers and sprinkle with pine nuts. Bake for approximately 5–10 minutes or until it becomes soft and gooey. This is sensational served with your favourite GF crackers.

Morning & Afternoon Teas

If in doubt, leave it out
If there's no doubt, you can pig out!

Graham Price, The Coeliac Society of Australia

1,1,1,1 Cake

A recipe from the poetic Belinda Gillam.

- *1 cup (120g) dessicated coconut*
- *1 cup (250ml) milk*
- *1 cup (200g) caster sugar*
- *1½ cups (250g) GF self raising flour*

Preheat oven to 180°C. Place all ingredients in a bowl and mix. Pour mixture into a baking paper lined loaf tin. Bake for 45 minutes.

Optional: If browning too fast on top, ¾ of the way through cooking, cover with a piece of aluminium foil.

Note: If using normal self raising flour, this cake requires just 1 cup, however using gluten free self raising flour, an additional ½ cup is required.

Almond Muffins

MAKES 12

You will be surprised how quick and easy these are.

- ¾ cup (125g) GF self raising flour, sifted
- ¼ cup (40g) almond meal
- 1¼ cup (300ml) double cream, not whipped
- 3 tbs. sugar

Preheat oven to 180°C. Place all ingredients in a bowl and mix until just combined. Dollop into greased or non-stick mini-muffin trays. Bake for 20 minutes or until golden brown.

Optional: Add fresh blueberries or raspberries or whatever fruit you have to the mix.

Almond Bread Slice

MAKES 15 SLICES

Recipe from Cyndi O'Meara.

- 4 free range egg whites
- ½ cup (100g) sugar
- 1 cup (175g) GF plain flour
- 160g almonds

Preheat oven to 180°C. Beat egg whites until stiff, then add sugar and beat for 1 minute. Stir in flour and almonds. Place mixture in a greased or lined loaf tin and bake for 40 minutes. When cool enough, slice thinly. Place slices on a baking tray and return to oven until browned (10–15 minutes).

Apple Slice

A recipe from the lovely Trudy Graham ... *This is dynamite!*

- *1 x GF pkt golden butter cake mix*
- *125g butter, melted*
- *420g can stewed apple*
- *200g sour cream*

Preheat oven to 180°C. Combine cake mix and butter and press into a paper lined baking dish. Cook for 15 minutes in oven. In a separate bowl, mix the tin of pie apple and sour cream.
After 15 minutes, remove base and top with apple mix. Return to oven for 15 minutes. Remove and allow to cook in the fridge before cutting.

Optional: Add 1 cup coconut to the base mix. Sprinkle the apple mix with cinnamon before baking.

Cashew Cream

MAKES ⅔ CUP

A recipe from Kim Morrison who says 'This makes a delicious change from cream on cakes, pancakes and desserts!'

- *120g cashew nuts, unsalted*
- *3 oranges, peeled and chopped*
- *1 apple, cored and peeled*
- *1 tbs. honey*

Place all ingredients in blender. Process until smooth and creamy. Serve cold.

Chocolate Dipped Lychees

A recipe from Meg Wilson. These are elegant, easy and amazing with coffee.

- *100g milk chocolate*
- *¼ cup (60ml) cream*
- *1½ cups fresh lychees, peeled and de-seeded*

Melt chocolate and add ¼ cup of cream, mix well. Dip lychees and pop onto a paper lined plate and set in fridge.

Optional: Can use tinned lychees — just drain and pat dry before dipping.

Chocolate and Coconut Clusters

MAKES 24

Recipe from Shirley Bermingham.

- *150g dark cooking chocolate*
- *100g GF cornflakes*
- *⅔ cup (80g) dessicated coconut*
- *½ cup white chocolate buttons*

Line a mini-muffin tray with little squares of baking paper or small fairy cake cases. Melt dark chocolate. Mix cornflakes and dessicated coconut and pour into chocolate stirring well spoon mixture into cases, top with choc buttons and set in fridge for at least 1 hour.

Citrus Frosting

MAKES ⅔ CUP

- *1 tbs. (15g) butter*
- *2–3 tbs. cream cheese*
- *1 tsp. lemon zest (optional)*
- *1–1½ cups (120g) GF icing sugar*

Soften butter. Add cream cheese and beat well. Add lemon zest and icing sugar (start with 1 cup and if you need more add slowly). Continue to beat until icing is nice and smooth.

Optional: Substitute orange for lemon.

Cookies and Cream Truffles

MAKES 24

Watch these fly!

- *180g pkt GF chocolate cream biscuits*
- *125g cream cheese*
- *125g chocolate*
- *2 tbs. cream*

In a food processor, crush cookies. Add cream cheese, processing until there are no traces of cream cheese. Remove mixture and roll into small balls, place on a plate and refrigerate for 45 minutes. Melt chocolate over a pan of simmering water. When melted stir in cream. Roll balls in chocolate mixture to coat. Refrigerate until set.

Optional: Can use GF chocolate chip or plain chocolate biscuits.

Cranberry Biscuits

MAKES 12

- 2 cups GF pancake mix
- ½ cup (125ml) milk
- ⅓ cup (70g) sugar
- ⅓ cup craisins

Preheat oven 200°C. Mix all ingredients, then drop a spoonful onto a baking paper lined tray. Bake 10–12 minutes or until just turning brown.

Note: These tend to cook faster than normal flour biscuits.

Optional: Substitute craisins for chocolate-chips.

Date Loaf

SERVES 6–8

A recipe from Mrs Frasier, Raceview QLD. *Absolutely divine!*

- 375g pkt dates
- 2 tsp. instant coffee
- 1 generous cup (175g) GF self raising flour
- ¼ cup flaked almonds

Preheat oven to 160°C. Add coffee to 1 cup of boiling water and mix. Pour over dates and soak overnight. Stir in GF flour. Pour mixture into a baking paper lined loaf tin, sprinkle with flaked almonds and bake for 45 minutes.

Optional: Serve warm with lashings of butter.

Espresso Amorettis

MAKES 24

- 1 tbs. instant coffee
- 3 free range egg whites
- 1 cup (200g) caster sugar
- 3 cups (500g) almond meal

Preheat oven to 160°C, dissolve coffee into 2 tbs. boiling water in a bowl. Allow the mixture to cool. Beat egg whites until stiff peaks form. Add egg whites, sugar and almond meal to coffee mix and stir until combined. Using a tablespoon, dollop the mixture into balls on a paper lined baking tray. Bake for 20 minutes or until just beginning to turn brown.

Flourless Chocolate Cake

- 4 free range eggs
- 1 cup (200g) caster sugar
- 200g butter
- 250g dark chocolate

Preheat oven 180°C. Separate eggs, add ½ the sugar to the yolks and beat well with a mixer. In a separate bowl, beat egg whites until fluffy then add remaining sugar, gradually beating until stiff peaks form. Melt butter and chocolate over hot water stirring regularly. Pour into egg yolk mixture and fold. Once combined fold in egg whites. Line a cake tin with greaseproof paper and pour in mixture. Bake for 40 minutes in the lower third of your oven.

Note: This cake will collapse as it has no flour to sustain the rise.

Optional: Can be served warm or cold and is delicious with fresh whipped cream.

Fruit Cake

SERVES 8

Recipe from Jen Whittington ... *S.e.n.s.a.t.i.o.n.a.l!*

- *1 kg dried mixed fruit*
- *2 cups (500ml) fruit juice or cold organic tea of choice*
- *2 cups (350g) GF self raising flour*

Preheat oven to 125°C. Soak fruits in juice/tea overnight. Stir flour into soaked fruit and mix well. Spoon mixture into a 22 cm lined cake tin. Bake for 2 – 2½ hours in the bottom of your oven or until cooked through. Remove and leave to cool. Place in an airtight container or wrap in aluminium foil.

Optional: Add a shot of your favourite tipple — sherry, brandy, rum, Grand Marnier.

Fruit Slice

MAKES 12

- *375g dried mixed fruit*
- *400g can condensed milk*
- *1¼ cups (215g) GF self raising flour*

Preheat oven to 160°C. Mix all ingredients together and pour into a baking paper lined tray. Bake for 40–45 minutes or until cooked when tested. Allow to cool and slice. Can be kept in freezer for up to one month.

Optional: For a flavour variation, add 1 cup of coconut to the mixture before baking. This is lovely served topped with your favourite icing.

Hazelnut Torte

SERVES 8

- *350g hazelnuts, finely ground (we used a blender)*
- *2 tsp. GF baking powder*
- *6 large free range eggs*
- *½ cup (100g) caster sugar*

Preheat the oven to 170°C. Line a 22 cm springform cake tin with baking paper. Reserve approx. 10 hazelnuts and place the rest in a blender then blend until very fine. Add baking powder and set aside. Separate egg yolks from egg whites and in a large bowl whip the egg yolks with the sugar until pale yellow in colour. Beat the ground hazelnut mixture into the egg yolk and sugar mixture. In another bowl, whisk the egg whites until stiff. Quickly fold ⅓ of the egg whites into the yolk mixture, then add the remaining whites and fold in until no streaks remain. Pour into cake tin and bake 60 to 75 minutes, or until top of cake springs back when lightly tapped. Cool on wire rack.

Optional: When cool, cut in half and spread generously with whipped cream and decorate with strawberries or coffee cream (see next recipe). Sprinkle with remaining nuts.

Mascarpone Icing

MAKES 1 CUP

- *125ml cream*
- *125g mascarpone*
- *2 tbs. GF icing sugar*
- *1 tsp. honey*

With a hand held mixer, mix all ingredients until thick and creamy. This is sensational served on the walnut cake ... *Yuummy!!*

Optional: Replace honey with fresh raspberries or blueberries or 1 tbs. instant coffee for a coffee cream.

Orange Coconut Clusters

MAKES 12

- *200g dark chocolate*
- *1 tsp. orange extract*
- *1 cup almonds, toasted and coarsely chopped*
- *1 cup shredded coconut, toasted*

In a medium saucepan, melt the chocolate over very low heat. Stir in the orange extract. Cool slightly then add almonds and coconut. Stir to coat. Drop heaped tablespoons of mixture onto a paper lined baking tray. Allow to cool in fridge.

Peanut Butter Cookies

MAKES AROUND 24 ... TRY THEM!

- *1 cup (260g) crunchy peanut butter*
- *1 cup (220g) brown sugar*
- *1 tsp. cinnamon*
- *1 large free range egg*

Preheat oven to 180°C. Mix all ingredients in a bowl. Using a tbs. roll the amount into small balls and pop onto 2 paper lined baking trays. Slightly flatten with a fork, crisscross style. Bake for 10 minutes or until a thin crust forms on the cookie.

Note: These will harden as they cool.

Pikelets

MAKES 10

- *1 egg*
- *1½ cups (260g) GF self raising flour*
- *4 tsp. sugar*
- *½ cup (125ml) milk*

Beat egg and sugar together before adding the other ingredients, mix thoroughly. Heat a non-stick frying pan and dollop a heaped tbs. of the mixture into the pan. Flip pikelet when you see small bubbles forming on its upper side. Cook for a further minute and repeat until the mixture is used. Serve with butter, cream, jam, fruit or syrup.

Pineapple Cake

SERVES 8

A recipe by Brett McCosker. 2 words — TRY IT!!!

- *2 generous cups (350g) GF self raising flour*
- *1 cup (200g) caster sugar*
- *450g can crushed pineapple*

Preheat oven to 180°C. Pop flour into a mixing bowl and combine with sugar. Add pineapple (entire contents of the can) and mix well. Pour into a baking paper lined 22 cm cake tin and bake for 40–50 minutes.

Pineapple Cake Icing

- *400g can condensed milk*
- *115g butter, melted*
- *1 cup (120g) shredded coconut*
- *½ tsp. vanilla essence*

Combine condensed milk and melted butter and bring to boil. Stirring constantly, boil for 4 minutes. Add coconut and mix. While mixture is hot, spread over cooled cake.

Hint: The above amounts cover the entire cake, lid and sides. If, however, you just want to cover the top, use half of the ingredients.

Quart Cake

SERVES 8

Recipe from Peter in the BBC studios in London.

- *3 free range eggs*
- *1 cup (230g) butter, softened*
- *1 cup (220g) muscovado sugar*
- *1 cup (175g) GF self raising flour*

Preheat oven to 180°C. Mix all ingredients together and place into a baking paper lined loaf tin. Bake for 45 minutes.

Raisin Loaf

A *fantastic* recipe from the quirky Kt Anbeck.

- *1 tbs. (15g) butter (a little extra for greasing)*
- *1 cup (200g) sugar*
- *1 cup (170g) raisins*
- *2 cups (350g) GF self raising flour*

Preheat oven to 180°C. Place butter, sugar and raisins in a saucepan with 1 cup water and bring to boil. Reduce heat and simmer for 5 minutes, set aside and allow to cool. Add GF flour and mix well. Bake in a greased loaf tin for 45 minutes.

Optional: Cut into thick slices and serve with butter.

Raspberry & Almond Cake

SERVES 12

- *2 cups frozen raspberries, thawed, juice included*
- *6 free range eggs*
- *1 cup (200g) caster sugar*
- *255g pkt almond meal*

Preheat oven to 160°C. Puree raspberries with their juice in a bowl. Beat eggs and sugar with an electric beater until light and fluffy, add puree and almond meal. Stir well, pour into greased 22 cm cake tin and bake for 60–70 minutes.

Optional: You can substitute raspberries with apples, bananas, oranges or mandarin. Topped with cream cheese icing and sprinkled with poppy seeds, this cake is BEEEEEUUUUUUUTIFUL!!

Rocky Road

A recipe by Jennette McCosker ... Kim's favourite!!

- *250g GF milk chocolate*
- *100g macadamia nuts, roughly chopped*
- *1 cup GF marshmallows*
- *1 cup GF Turkish delight, roughly chopped*

Break chocolate into pieces and melt in microwave on medium high, stirring every 20 seconds. Allow to cool slightly before adding remaining ingredients. Mix until well combined. Line a small rectangular dish with baking paper, pour the mixture into it, neaten edges and refrigerate until set. Cut into desired serving pieces.

Optional: Use nut of choice — almond, hazelnut, Brazil nut etc.

Scones

MAKES 12

- *4 cups (700g) GF self raising flour*
- *2 tsp. GF baking powder*
- *300ml single cream*
- *1 cup (250ml) lemonade*

Preheat oven to 200°C. Sift self raising flour into a bowl, make a well and pour in cream and ¾ of the lemonade. Mix to make a firm dough (if too wet, add more flour), roll onto a floured surface and knead into a high, round mound. Cut with a scone cutter and place on a paper lined baking tray close together. Bake for 15 minutes or until golden brown.

Hint: For 'savoury scones' substitute the lemonade for soda water and add semi-dried tomatoes or parmesan cheese or your favourite herbs to flavour.

Shortbread

MAKES 16

- 1 cup (175g) rice flour
- ½ cup (60g) maize cornflour
- ½ cup (60g) GF icing sugar
- 170g butter, softened

Preheat oven to 180°C. Sift flours, add sugar and butter and mix with hands until a soft dough forms. Roll into a log shape and refrigerate for 1 hour. Remove from fridge and slice in ½ cm thick pieces. Arrange on a lined baking tray, allowing room for spreading. Bake for 20–25 minutes or until golden.

Optional: Sprinkle with caster sugar before baking. Roll into 2 cm balls, and at Christmas time press half a glazed cherry onto it prior to baking.

Sponge Cake

SERVES 8

- ¾ cup (90g) maize cornflour
- 1 tsp. GF baking powder
- 3 eggs, separated
- ½ cup (100g) caster sugar

Preheat oven 180°C. Sift cornflour and baking powder with a pinch of salt. Beat egg whites with an electric mixer until stiff peaks are starting to form. Beat in egg yolks. Gradually beat in sugar until mixture is light, beating for around 10 minutes. Pour mixture into a paper lined (or greased) 22cm cake tin and bake for 20-25 minutes. Remove from the pan and cool on wire rack.

Optional: When ready to serve top with freshly whipped cream and freshly chopped strawberries.

Sweet Pastry

SERVES 6

- ½ cup (60g) maize cornflour
- ¾ cup (185ml) milk
- 1½ cups (180g) dessicated coconut
- 120g melted butter

Simply mix and press into a dish. This is good for sweet pies, tarts and cheesecakes.

Walnut Cake

SERVES 8

THIS IS BRILLIANT!

- 4 large free range eggs, separated
- 1 cup (200g) caster sugar
- 1 lemon
- 350g walnuts, finely ground (we used a blender)

Preheat the oven to 160°C. Line a 22 cm springform cake tin with baking paper. Using an electric beater, beat the egg yolks and sugar together until light and fluffy (approx. 5 minutes). Grate the zest of the entire lemon into the mixture and stir. In a separate bowl, beat the egg whites until stiff peaks form. Fold one third of the whites into the egg yolk mixture. Add the ground walnuts, stirring until thoroughly blended. Carefully fold in the remaining egg whites to maintain a light texture. Pour the mixture into the tin and bake for about 50–60 minutes until firm and golden brown. Allow to cool before removing from the tin.

Optional: Serve with freshly whipped mascarpone icing.

White Choc Macaroons

MAKES 16

- 2 free range eggs, separated
- ¾ cup (150g) caster sugar
- 2 cups (240g) dessicated coconut
- 1 cup (100g) coarsely grated white chocolate

Preheat oven to 160°C. Beat egg whites in small bowl with an electric mixer until soft peaks form. Gradually add the egg yolks and then the sugar, beating until sugar has dissolved. Stir in coconut and chocolate. Roll 2 tsp. of mix into balls and place about 3 cm apart on a non-stick, paper lined oven tray. Cook for 20 minutes or until golden brown. Stand biscuits for 5 minutes before transferring to a wire rack to cool.

Optional: Rachel Kelly suggested substituting the white chocolate for the zest of a lime, making 'Coconut & Lime Macaroons!'

Light Meals & Lunches

If every day is an awakening, you will never grow old —
You will just keep on growing.

Gail Sheehy

Soups

Asparagus Soup

SERVES 4

- *2 bunches asparagus, washed, woody ends removed*
- *4 cups (1ltr.) chicken or vegetable GF stock*
- *½ cup (125ml) double cream*
- *Cayenne pepper to taste*

Cut the asparagus into 2–3 cm pieces and set aside. In a large, non-stick saucepan, pour stock and add asparagus, bring to a simmer. Cook for 5 minutes or until the asparagus is tender, but still green. Remove from heat and puree using a hand held blender. Return to low heat, add the cream and cook on low until heated through. Season to taste with sea salt and cayenne pepper. Ladle the soup into bowls and serve hot.

Tip: When buying asparagus, it is fresh when it snaps, not bends. And where it snaps naturally, indicates the difference between the good part (the spear) and the end which is fibrous, tough and stringy.

Bacon & Pea Soup

SERVES 4–6

This is really tasty!

- *1 kg bacon bones*
- *200g pkt dried peas*
- *2 onions, roughly chopped*

Place all ingredients in a large saucepan with 10 cups water. Bring to boil and then simmer for 1 hour. Remove from heat and allow the soup to cool. Remove bacon from bones and add water if the soup is too thick. Blend and serve with your favourite GF bread.

Carrot & Coriander Soup

SERVES 8

This is very popular in the UK.

- *2 ltr. GF vegetable stock*
- *1 large onion, chopped*
- *6 stems fresh coriander, roots included*
- *8 organic carrots, roughly chopped*

Heat vegetable stock gently and add roughly chopped coriander leaves and roots, onion and carrots. Bring to the boil, reduce heat and simmer until the carrots are tender. Season with pepper before blending.

Optional: Before serving, swirl some sour cream through if desired.

Chorizo & Pepper Soup

THIS SERVES 4–6 AND IS *REALLLLLLLY* TASTY!

- *2 GF chorizo sausages, diced*
- *4 red peppers, diced*
- *410g can whole peeled tomatoes*
- *750ml GF chicken stock*

Fry chorizo in a non-stick pan for 5 minutes, remove from pan and pat dry with absorbent paper before setting aside. Into the same pan with chorizo juices add peppers and fry for 5 minutes before adding tomatoes. Mix well, season with sea salt and pepper, add stock and bring to boil. Reduce heat and simmer until peppers are tender. Puree the soup and serve with chorizo pieces.

Corn & Chicken Soup

SERVES 4

Recipe from Michelle Ashdown.

- *4 cups (1ltr.) GF chicken stock*
- *500g of chicken breasts, sliced thinly*
- *2 x 420g cans of GF creamed corn*
- *4 free range eggs, lightly beaten*

Bring chicken stock to the boil in large non-stick saucepan. Add chicken, reduce and simmer for 3 minutes before adding the creamed corn. Simmer for 8 minutes and whisk in eggs. Continue to stir until egg is separated and spread evenly throughout the soup. Season with sea salt and pepper. Serve warm with GF toast.

Curried Pumpkin Soup

SERVES 4

- 1 kg pumpkin, peeled and chopped
- 1 generous tsp. GF curry powder
- 1 clove garlic, crushed
- 150ml double cream

Place pumpkin, curry and garlic in a saucepan and add 2 cups of water. Bring to boil, then reduce heat and simmer for 20 minutes or until pumpkin is tender. Blend before adding cream, stir the cream through and serve.

Easy Pumpkin Soup

SERVES 4 AND IS SO EASY.

- 1 pumpkin
- 410ml can evaporated milk
- 3 tbs. chopped parsley

Cook the pumpkin in boiling water until tender. Drain and mash, gradually add the evaporated milk until it is a soupy consistency. Season to taste and garnish with a sprinkle of chopped parsley. Serve with hot toast or croutons.

Hint: Give pumpkin soup a lift by stirring in a ¼ cup crunchy peanut butter and a handful of chopped coriander to each litre of soup.

Pumpkin, Lentil & Ginger Soup

SERVES 4

- ½ cup red lentils, rinsed
- 1 kg butternut pumpkin, cut into chunks
- 1 tbs. grated ginger
- 4 cups (1ltr.) GF vegetable stock

Place all ingredients into a large saucepan, season with sea salt and pepper if you like and cook on a medium heat for 30 minutes. Blend and serve.

Thai Pumpkin Soup

SERVES 4

A recipe from Anthony 'Spud' Moore. THAI-RRIFIC!!

- 1 kg butternut pumpkin, peeled and diced
- 2 tbs. GF red curry paste
- 300ml coconut cream
- 8 stems fresh coriander, chopped

Sauté pumpkin and red curry paste until it starts to catch on the saucepan. Add coconut cream to deglaze the pan, top with enough water to be level with the pumpkin and bring to boil. Reduce heat, simmering until the pumpkin becomes soft and mushy. Puree, season with sea salt and pepper and fold in chopped coriander.

Tomato Soup

SERVES 4

A recipe from the lovely Michelle Dodd who says, 'This is a deliciously, rich flavoured soup!'

- *8–12 plum tomatoes*
- *¼ cup (60ml) olive oil*
- *4 sprigs thyme*
- *2 cups (500ml) GF vegetable stock*

Preheat oven to 150°C. Cut plum tomatoes in half. Using a pastry brush, brush each with olive oil. Sprinkle over thyme leaves and season with sea salt and pepper. Roast for 30–45 minutes. Blend roasted tomatoes with vegie stock and heat through!

Tomato & Basil Soup

SERVES 4

A recipe from Marie McColl.

- *3 x 400g cans plum tomatoes*
- *2 cups (500ml) GF vegetable stock*
- *½ bunch fresh basil leaves*
- *2 tbs. brown sugar*

Place all ingredients in a saucepan, season with pepper and gently bring to the boil. Blend and serve in bowls.

Vegetable Croutons

SERVES 4

A recipe by Lorraine Leeson.

- ¼ cup (60ml) olive oil
- 1 small sweet potato or parsnip, peeled and diced
- 1 clove garlic

Heat oil in a large pan. Add the vegetables and garlic and cook for 10 minutes or until tender and lightly browned. Drain on paper and sprinkle over soup.

Hint: If any of your hot soups end up slightly salty, add to it a whole, peeled potato and simmer for about 15 minutes to absorb salt. Remove the potato and serve.

Optional: AJ Gregory says this is fantastic sprinkled over a salad.

Vegetable Gazpacho

SERVES 4

- 7 ripe plum tomatoes, cut in half
- ½ a continental cucumber, chopped
- ½ bunch fresh coriander
- ½ cup (125ml) red wine vinegar

In a food processor, blend all ingredients for a minute. Season to taste. To serve pour into 4 Martini glasses and garnish with fresh sprigs of coriander.

All Others

The easiest way to predict the future is to create it.

Anonymous

Bacon & Egg Quiches

MAKES 15

Recipe by AJ Gregory.

- 5 free range eggs
- 5 bacon rashers, rind removed and finely sliced
- 250ml single cream
- 6 button mushrooms, sliced

Preheat 185°C. Fry bacon in a non-stick frying pan till lightly golden brown. Tip onto absorbent paper to remove excess fat. Mix eggs and cream together then add mushrooms and bacon. Evenly spoon mixture into a silicon mini-muffin tray. Bake for 7–8 minutes or until lightly golden brown. Turn out and serve.

* Optional Fillings: *Finely chopped leek (high in anti-oxidants)*

                                   Finely chopped spring onion

                                    Parsley

                                    Pine nuts

                                    Feta

                                    Top with a small, roasted cherry tomato

Baked Peppers

SERVES 2

- 2 red peppers, halved and deseeded
- 2 cups leftover bolognaise sauce
- 80g grated parmesan cheese

Place peppers on a paper lined baking tray and fill with bolognaise. Top with parmesan and bake in a 180°C oven for 20 minutes.

Optional: Delicious served with a fresh green salad.

Note: The difference between red, yellow and green peppers is red are ripe, yellow are nearly ripe and green aren't!

Beef Koftas

MAKES 4–6

- ½ cup (130g) crunchy peanut butter
- 2 tsp. GF curry powder
- 1 free range egg
- 500g lean beef mince

Warm peanut butter in the microwave on high for 30 seconds to soften. Mix in curry powder and egg. Add to mince and combine. Roll mixture into fat sausage shapes using ½ cup of mixture for each kofta. Grill or BBQ until cooked.

Optional: Serve as a burger or on GF bread with GF satay sauce and salad or separately as a patty with vegetables … Mmmmm!

Cheese & Garlic Pizza

SERVES 2

A recipe from Anthony 'Spud' Moore.

- *3 GF tortilla rounds*
- *16 cloves garlic*
- *100g parmesan cheese, grated*
- *100g mozzarella, grated*

Preheat oven 230°C. Peel garlic, wrap in aluminium foil and roast in oven for 15 minutes. Remove and cool. Lay one tortilla flat and spread ⅓ garlic, ⅓ parmesan and ⅓ mozzarella. Lay second tortilla on top and repeat process, lay third tortilla on top and repeat process. Cook for 15 minutes or until cheese bubbles and turns golden brown.

Easy Aubergine Grill

MAKES 2

This is a glorious lunch served with a fresh green salad.

- *370g aubergine, cut into 8 thick slices*
- *2 tsp. olive oil*
- *1 cup GF tomato pasta sauce, heated*
- *50g cheddar cheese, grated*

Preheat grill. Brush each aubergine slice with oil and place on a single layer of aluminium foil-lined baking tray. Season with sea salt and pepper and grill for 3 minutes or until golden. Turn each slice and grill for another 3 minutes. Spoon the sauce onto each slice and sprinkle with cheese, grill again for 3 minutes or until cheese is golden.

Gourmet Pizza

MAKES 4

- 4 GF wraps
- 4 generous tsp. GF basil pesto
- 8 slices GF salami or paper-thin GF ham, torn
- 100g mozzarella cheese, grated

Place the wraps under a hot grill for 1 minute. Remove and on the untoasted side spread with pesto, evenly top with ham and sprinkle with cheese. Season with pepper. Return to the grill for 3–4 minutes or until the cheese has melted and turned golden brown.

Homestyle Baked Beans

SERVES 4–6

- 2 tbs. olive oil
- 1 large yellow pepper, chopped
- 2 x 400g cans mixed beans
- 2 x 400g cans crushed tomatoes with herbs and garlic

Heat a medium sized pot and add oil, sauté pepper until just soft, add beans and tomato. Season with sea salt and pepper and simmer for 20 minutes on low heat stirring occasionally.

Jacket Potato with Tomato Salsa

SERVES 1

- *1 large potato (200g)*
- *2 tbs. tomato salsa*
- *¼ cup low fat cottage cheese*
- *1 tbs. chopped fresh chives*

Preheat oven to 180°C. Pierce potato with knife several times. Wrap potato in aluminium foil, bake for 30–40 minutes, or until soft. Remove from oven, stand for 5 minutes, remove foil and cut a crisscross halfway into the potato. Add cottage cheese, top with salsa and sprinkle with chives.

* Optional Fillings: *GF Taco sauce, sour cream and mashed avocado*

Tuna, GF coleslaw and grated cheese

Chilli con carne, sour cream and chives

GF baked beans and grated cheese

GF korma sauce, sour cream and coriander

Quesadillas

SERVES 4

- *1 tbs. (15g) butter*
- *8 medium GF corn tortillas*
- *2 vine-ripened tomatoes, sliced*
- *100g cheddar cheese, grated*

Melt butter in a non-stick frying pan over medium heat. Lay 4 tortillas on a clean, flat surface and top with tomatoes and cheese. Season with sea salt and pepper before placing remaining tortillas on top. Cook over medium heat for 2 minutes or until bottom tortilla is crisp and golden. Flip and repeat. Cut into wedges to serve.

Optional: Dollop some GF; mango chutney, tomato relish or mustard of choice before frying.

* Optional Fillings: Refried beans, red chilli sauce and grated cheese

Cheese and fresh basil

Avocado, chicken and mozzarella

Spicy mince, 3 bean mix, diced tomato and coriander

Toasted Camembert Sandwich

MAKES 2

- *4 slices GF bread*
- *1 tbs. (15g) butter*
- *125g wheel of camembert cheese, thickly sliced*
- *2 tbs. cranberry sauce*

Butter one side of each slice of bread. Cut ¾ of the cheese into thick slices and lay on the unbuttered side of the bread. Dollop each with a spoonful of cranberry sauce. Top with remaining slices of bread, butter side up. Fry in a non-stick pan for a couple of minutes on each side, pressing down with an egg flipper to flatten. When cheese is warm and melting, remove, cut and serve immediately … *Yummy!*

Optional: For a taste variation drizzle the cheese and cranberry with a little balsamic vinegar before toasting.

Salmon & Camembert Omelette

SERVES 6

A recipe from the very generous Marie McColl.

- *8 free range eggs*
- *1 tsp. butter*
- *150g pkt smoked salmon*
- *125g wheel camembert cheese*

Beat eggs with ⅓ cup (80ml) water in a bowl. Season with sea salt and pepper. Grease lightly a small non-stick frying pan with a little of the butter. Add ½ cup of the egg mixture, tilting the pan for an even coverage. Cook for 2 minutes or until just set. Place ¼ of the salmon and cheese over half the omelette, fold over the other half and cook until cheese just starts to melt. Repeat the process 3 more times.

Optional: Replace the smoked salmon with a can of pink salmon, drained and flaked and substitute camembert with grated tasty cheese.

Salt & Pepper Calamari

SERVES 6 Y.U.M.M.Y!

- *1 tsp. Sichuan peppercorns and 1 tsp. sea salt*
- *400g fresh calamari*
- *1 cup (125g) maize cornflour*
- *1 cup (250ml) sunflower oil*

In a dry pan, roast the peppercorns until they become fragrant and begin to crackle, transfer to a mortar along with sea salt and grind. Add cornflour and roll the calamari in the mixture, shake off any excess. Deep fry in a hot wok for 1 minute or until cooked. Drain and serve hot.

Spicy Chorizo Wrap

SERVES 2

- 1 GF chorizo sausage, *chopped into small pieces*
- 3 free range eggs, *beaten*
- 2 GF wraps
- ½ punnet watercress

Brown chorizo in a medium non-stick frying pan and sauté for 2–3 minutes. Remove, season eggs before pouring into the same pan (utilising the flavour and oil from the chorizo) cook until bubbles appear, add chorizo and flip after a minute. When set, lay omelette on tortilla. Scatter with cress. Wrap tightly and cut in half.

Summer Rolls

SERVES 4

- 400g minced pork
- ⅓ cup (80ml) GF oyster sauce
- 8 rice-paper rolls
- 60g mange tout, *sliced*

Heat a non-stick frying pan and brown pork. Season with sea salt and pepper before stirring in oyster sauce. Remove from heat and allow to cool. Take each rice wrapper and lay it in water for 20 seconds. Remove and place on a cutting board. Place an ⅛ of the mince down one edge of each wrapper and top with a generous serve of slices of mange tout. Roll up tucking in the ends as you go to secure the content. Cut in half and serve immediately.

Optional: Serve with some GF sweet chilli sauce to dip.

Tip: Don't be tempted to overfill as we first did as the rice paper will split.

Tandoori Wings

D.e.l.i.c.i.o.u.s

- ⅓ cup (85g) GF tandoori paste
- ⅓ cup (80g) yoghurt
- 1 medium brown onion, grated
- 1 kg chicken wings

Preheat oven to 200°C. Combine paste, yoghurt and onion in large bowl. Add chicken and coat generously. Cover and refrigerate for at least 3 hours. Place chicken on an oiled wire rack set inside larger shallow baking dish. Roast, uncovered, for 30 minutes, or until chicken is well browned and cooked through.

Tostadas

SERVES 4

- 4 GF tortillas
- ½ cup (85g) chunky tomato salsa
- 425g can Mexe-beans, drained
- 100g cheddar cheese, grated

Preheat oven to 200°C. Line 2 baking trays with baking paper. Place tortillas on trays and spread thickly with salsa. Combine beans and cheese in a bowl, mix and then spoon evenly over each tortilla. Bake for 10 minutes or until tortillas are golden and crisp.

Optional: Top with Guacamole (see dips).

Zucchini (Courgette) Slice

SERVES 8

- *3 courgettes, grated*
- *4 bacon rashers, finely diced*
- *1 cup (175g) GF self raising flour*
- *6 eggs, beaten*

Preheat oven 180°C. Mix all ingredients together and season well. Pour mixture into a 16 x 26cm baking dish and bake for 25-30 minutes. Serve hot, sliced into long fingers.

Optional: Sprinkle with grated cheddar cheese before baking.

Salads

Don't sweat the small stuff, it's ALL small stuff.

Anthony Robbins

Asparagus with Macadamia & Cranberry Dressing

SERVES 4

- *2 bunches asparagus, trimmed*
- *50g roasted macadamias, finely chopped*
- *⅓ cup dried cranberries, finely chopped*
- *¼ cup (60ml) red wine vinegar*

Cook asparagus in a large saucepan of boiling water for 2–3 minutes or until bright green. Drain. Rinse under cold water. Lay out on a platter. Meanwhile, toss the macadamias and cranberries in a non-stick frying pan, when warmed add the red wine vinegar and stir to combine. Gently spoon the mixture over the asparagus.

Basil & Lentil Salad

SERVES 6 ... This is faaaaaaaaaaaaabulous!

- *2 fresh bunches of basil*
- *400g can of brown lentils, drained*
- *1 punnet of cherry tomatoes, halved*
- *½ Spanish onion, thinly sliced*

Tear basil leaves from stem and place in a salad bowl. Add remaining ingredients and toss to combine.

Optional: Serve drizzled with the Classic Salad Dressing (see Salad Dressings).

Hint: Basil leaves are best torn or used whole rather than cut with a knife as they bruise easily. The herb is best used raw as cooking diminishes its flavour.

Caprice Salad

SERVES 4

This is a tasty northern Italian salad named after the region it originated in!

- *6 vine ripened tomatoes, cut into thick slices*
- *2 tbs. (30ml) extra virgin olive oil*
- *100g fresh buffalo mozzarella, thickly sliced*
- *½ bunch fresh basil leaves, leaves only*

Arrange tomato slices on a large flat serving plate, don't mind if they overlap. Drizzle with oil and top with slices of bocconcini and basil. Season generously with sea salt and pepper, cover and chill before serving.

Note: This salad is best eaten listening to a Frank Sinatra CD and with a glass of wine!

Carrot, Sultana & Celery Salad

SERVES 6

- *4 carrots, peeled and grated*
- *1 cup (170g) sultanas*
- *2 celery stalks, thinly sliced*
- *¼ cup (65g) GF mayonnaise*

Mix all ingredients together and chill before serving.

Optional: Substitute celery for fresh pineapple.

Cherry Tomato & Cucumber Salad

SERVES 6

- *100g pkt mixed salad leaves*
- *250g punnet cherry tomatoes, halved*
- *1 cucumber, thinly sliced*
- *¼ cup (60ml) balsamic and roasted garlic salad dressing*

Combine first 3 ingredients in a serving dish and drizzle with dressing. Toss gently to combine.

Optional: Any balsamic based salad dressing is nice.

Tip: To make cucumber ribbons use a vegetable peeler.

Chicken Salad

SERVES 4

A recipe from Lisa Darr.

- 1 boneless skinless chicken breast, grilled
- ½ cup green grapes, halved
- 2–3 celery stalks, thinly sliced
- 2 tbs. orange juice

Slice the chicken breast to desired thickness. Combine chicken, grapes and celery in a large bowl and toss well. Drizzle orange juice over salad and season with sea salt and pepper.

Dijonnaise Eggs

SERVES 6

A recipe from Marie McColl.

- 6 hard boiled free range eggs
- 2 tsp. chopped parsley
- 1–2 tbs. GF Dijonnaise

Spoon yolks out of eggs into a bowl and mash with a fork, stir in parsley and enough Dijonnaise to give a soft consistency. Spoon mixture back into egg cases and refrigerate. Serve garnished with parsley and seasoned with sea salt and pepper.

Feta & Watermelon Salad

SERVES 6

- ½ watermelon
- 2 tbs. mint leaves, finely chopped
- 1 onion, finely chopped
- 50g feta cheese

Cut watermelon into chunky cubes and remove seeds. Add mint and onion and mix. When ready to serve drain excess juice and place in a serving bowl. Sprinkle with feta cheese.

Optional: Serve drizzled with caramelised balsamic vinegar.

Green Bean Salad

SERVES 4–6

- 250g green beans, topped and tailed
- 2 large vine-ripened tomatoes
- 60g walnuts, chopped
- ¼ cup (60ml) balsamic vinegar

Place beans in a microwave container, cover with water and microwave for 4 minutes or until just tender. Drain and place on a serving plate. Top with chopped tomato, sprinkle with walnuts and drizzle with balsamic vinegar.

Optional: Caramelised balsamic vinegar is really nice too.

Pea & Mint Salad

SERVES 4

- *2 cups mange tout*
- *2 tbs. fresh mint, chopped*
- *100g feta cheese, crumbled*
- *2 tbs. (30ml) fresh lemon juice*

Place mange tout in a serving dish and allow them to sit in boiling water for 2 minutes. Drain and rinse under cold water, allow to dry. Add mint and feta. Drizzle with juice and toss gently to combine.

Potato Salad

SERVES 4

A recipe from the ever helpful Cathy DiBella ... *Yuuuuumy!*

- *8 desiree potatoes, washed and cut into chunks*
- *⅓ cup (100g) sour cream*
- *⅓ cup (85g) GF mayonnaise*
- *1 tbs. GF wholegrain mustard*

Boil potatoes for approx. 8 minutes or until soft when pierced, remove and allow to cool. Combine remaining 3 ingredients and chill. Toss potatoes through salad dressing when ready to serve.

Optional: Finely dice some celery, spring onions or whatever vegetables you have into the mix.

Prawn & Mango Salad

SERVES 4

- *12 large peeled, de-veined and cooked prawns*
- *1 large mango, peeled and sliced*
- *1 cucumber, sliced finely and lengthways*
- *120g roasted cashews, unsalted*

Mix all ingredients lightly. Squeeze juice from the mango and lightly toss throughout the salad and serve ... Quick, easy and delicious!

Roast Pumpkin & Fig Salad

SERVES 4

Recipe by the lovely Carolyn Thomson.

- *100g pkt baby spinach*
- *120g pumpkin, sliced and roasted*
- *120g dried figs*
- *60g walnuts,chopped*

Arrange pumpkin and figs on spinach and sprinkle with walnuts.

Optional: Drizzle generously with caramelised balsamic vinegar ... Mmmmm!

Rocket & Parmesan Salad

SERVES 4

A recipe from the clever Cheyne McCorkindale.

- *120g pkt baby rocket*
- *½ Spanish onion, finely sliced*
- *50g parmesan cheese, finely grated*
- *1 tbs. extra virgin olive oil*

Combine rocket and oil in a serving bowl. Add onion and parmesan and mix well, ensuring an even coating of parmesan across the rocket. Serve and enjoy!

Salmon & Caper Salad

SERVES 4

- *100g can drained salmon*
- *100g feta, crumbled*
- *120g baby rocket*
- *1 tbs. drained capers, chopped*

Simply mix and enjoy!

Summer Salad

SERVES 4

A little beauty created by Rachael to get Jaxson to eat salad!!

- *120g pkt mixed lettuce*
- *200g strawberries, hulled and quartered*
- *50g mange tout*
- *2 fresh mangoes – skin removed, flesh sliced, but reserve the seed*

Wash all ingredients and drain excess water. Place lettuce into a serving bowl with strawberries, mange tout and mango slices. Squeeze juice from around the mango seed over the top of the salad, lightly toss throughout and serve.

Sweet Salad

SERVES 4

A recipe by Chef Dan Primmer.

- *500g sweet potato peeled and diced*
- *2 large corn cobs*
- *6 tbs. honey*
- *½ cup (125g) natural Greek yoghurt*

Preheat oven to 160°C. Mix sweet potato, corn and honey, place on a paper lined baking tray and bake for 10 minutes or until sweet potato is soft. Remove from heat and allow to cool. Pop into serving bowl and coat with yoghurt, serve immediately.

Sweet Chilli Chicken Salad

SERVES 2–4

A recipe from Glen Turnbull.

- *2 cups leftover chicken, shredded*
- *½ a lettuce, shredded*
- *2 tbs. GF sweet chilli sauce*
- *1 tbs. GF mayonnaise*

Pop chicken and lettuce into a bowl. Mix sweet chilli and mayo together and combine well.

Optional: Add some thinly sliced Spanish onion.

Thai Chilli Mango Squid Salad

SERVES 4

A recipe from Spud Moore. "This is the tastiest salad ever!" Rach.

- *500g squid cleaned*
- *250ml GF Thai chilli sauce*
- *1 large ripe mango*
- *2 handfuls rocket*

Cut squid tubes into triangles. Marinate with Thai chilli sauce for 1 hour. De-seed and skin the mango, slice and place in a serving bowl. Pan fry squid quickly and add to mango, top with rocket and serve.

Waldorf Salad

SERVES 4

- 4 cups seasonal apples, diced
- ¾ cup (125g) raisins
- 60g pecan nuts, chopped
- ½ cup (130g) GF mayonnaise

In a bowl, combine ingredients and refrigerate until ready to serve.

Watermelon Salad

SERVES 4

- ½ seedless watermelon, cubed
- ½ bunch of watercress sprigs
- 6 fresh mint stems, leaves only, chopped
- 2 tbs. lemon juice

Place watermelon into a bowl, sprinkle with watercress and mint, toss lightly and then drizzle with lemon juice.

Note: 90% of a watermelon is (you guessed it) water, so it is a great hydrator for children in those warm summer months.

Potato

One cannot think well, love well, sleep well, if one has not dined well.

Virginia Woolf

Bombay Potatoes

SERVES 6

- *8–10 small potatoes, cut in half*
- *2 x 400g can chopped tomatoes*
- *3 tbs. GF garam masala curry powder*
- *½ cup (125g) natural yoghurt*

Preheat oven to 180°C. Place potatoes in a large baking paper lined dish. Pour tomatoes into a bowl and mix with garam masala. Pour mixture over potatoes and bake for 40–45 minutes or until tender. Serve dolloped with yoghurt .

Crunchy Wedges

SERVES 5

These are gooooooooooooooood!

- *2 large washed potatoes*
- *⅓ cup (80ml) olive oil*
- *2 cups (240g) GF cornflakes, crushed*
- *1 tbs. mixed herbs*

Preheat oven to 200°C. Cut potatoes into wedge shapes and place in a large bowl. Drizzle oil until all wedges are covered. Mix cornflakes and herbs and coat generously. Place on flat baking paper lined tray. Cook for 20 minutes and then turn and cook for a further 15 minutes.

Optional: Can also use sweet potato. Add parmesan cheese and paprika for an extra zing. Yum!!

Crispy Parmesan Wedges

SERVES 4

- *4 medium potatoes*
- *½ cup (125ml) olive oil*
- *50g parmesan cheese, grated*

Preheat oven to 180°C. Peel potatoes, cut a small slice off the bottom of each so that the potatoes sit flat. Place flat side down in baking dish, brush well with oil and bake for 20 minutes, brush occasionally with oil during cooking time. Sprinkle with parmesan cheese, bake further 20 minutes or until potatoes are crisp outside and tender inside. Do not turn potatoes during baking.

Garlic Potato

SERVES 4

- 4 large potatoes, peeled and cut into 1 cm slices
- 100g mozzarella cheese, grated — reserve ½ cup
- 2 cloves garlic, crushed
- 1 cup (320g) sour cream

Preheat oven 180°C. Lightly steam potatoes for 10 minutes, or until just soft — set aside. Combine cheese, garlic and sour cream in a bowl. In a baking dish, alternate one layer of potatoes with garlic, sour cream and cheese, ending with the liquid combo. Top with reserved cheese and bake in oven for 30–40 minutes.

Healthy Rustic Chips

SERVES 4

- 4 medium potatoes
- 1 tbs. olive oil

Heat oven to 220°C. Wash potatoes and cut into 2 cm thick chips. Boil until just tender. Drain and pat completely dry with absorbent paper. Toss potato in a large bowl with olive oil then place in a single layer on an oven tray. Roast uncovered for about 25 minutes or until browned.

Optional: Add a pinch of paprika before baking.

Mashed Potato

SERVES 4

- *4 potatoes, peeled and cubed*
- *1 clove garlic, crushed*
- *2 tbs. (30g) butter*
- *½ cup (125ml) milk*

Boil potatoes for 5 minutes or until soft, then drain. Add remaining ingredients and mash until smooth. Season with sea salt and pepper to serve.

Potato Cakes

MAKES 10

A Recipe by Carol Logan.

- *2 cups mashed potato*
- *2 cups diced, cooked bacon*
- *½ cup chopped spring onions*
- *1 pkt GF creamy chicken and vegetable soup*

Mix all together and roll into patties. Fry in a non-stick frying pan until brown on both sides.

Potato Scallops

SERVES 4

- 4 large potatoes
- 2 cups (350g) GF self raising flour
- ¾ cup (185ml) sunflower oil

Peel and wash potatoes, cut into thin slices and dry well. Sift flour into bowl and season, make a well in the centre, gradually add 1 cup (250ml) water to make a thick batter, beat until free of lumps. Coat potato slices lightly with extra flour, shake off excess. Dip each slice into batter and drain off excess before frying. Heat oil in large pan and deep fry slices until lightly golden. Drain on absorbent paper and sprinkle with sea salt.

Puffed Sweet Potato

SERVES 4

- 2 tbs. (30g) butter
- ½ cup (125ml) milk
- 2 cups mashed sweet potato
- 1 egg

Preheat oven 180°C. Melt 1 tbs. butter and to it add milk, season generously. Beat mixture into sweet potato, separate white from yolk of egg, add yolk to potato and beat well. Beat egg white until stiff peaks form and fold through mixture. Use 1 tbs. butter to grease a mini-muffin tray and dollop mixture into moulds and bake for 25 minutes.

Rosemary and Thyme Roast Spuds

SERVES 6

- 5 large scrubbed, peeled potatoes cut into thick wedges
- 4 tbs. olive oil
- 8 sprigs fresh rosemary
- 8 sprigs fresh thyme

Preheat oven to 200°C. Toss spuds in oil and sprinkle with fresh herbs and some sea salt if you prefer. Roast for 35–40 minutes, turning to ensure the wedges are evenly brown.

Sautéed Lemon Potatoes

SERVES 4

A recipe from Michelle Dodd ... These are sensational!

- 4 medium potatoes
- 3 tbs. (45ml) olive oil
- 1 tbs. (15g) butter
- ½ cup (125ml) lemon juice

Peel and cut potatoes into eighths, parboil for 3 minutes. Heat oil, butter and lemon juice in baking dish in a hot oven. Toss potatoes in pan, basting with liquid, and cook for 15–20 minutes or until golden.

Optional: Add freshly ground garlic to oil and lemon juice.

Sweet Potato Fritters

A recipe by Annabelle Taylor.

- *1 large sweet potato, peeled and grated*
- *3 tbs. GF mango chutney*
- *1 egg, lightly beaten*
- *2 cups (240g) rice flour (or GF breadcrumbs)*

Combine all ingredients in bowl. Fry in a non-stick frying pan until golden.

Optional: These are delicious served with satay sauce (see Sauces).

Tennessee Taters

SERVES 4

- *4 washed potatoes*
- *2 tsp. butter*
- *1 cup grated tasty cheese*
- *4 slices bacon, diced and fried*

Preheat oven to 180°C. Wrap potatoes in aluminium foil and bake for 40 minutes or until soft through. Cut large crosses in each, push potato towards centre so split opens wide, place ½ tsp. butter in each and divide cheese evenly, pushing down firmly. Sprinkle with bacon and pop under a grill until cheese melts.

Vegetables

Vegetables are a must on a diet. I suggest carrot cake, courgette bread, and pumpkin pie.

Jim Davis

Aioli Broccoli

SERVES 4

- *1 large bunch broccoli*
- *2 tbs. (30ml) olive oil*
- *2 tbs. (30g) butter*
- *2 cloves garlic, crushed*

Cut broccoli into chunky pieces, keeping 3–4 cm of the stem, and steam for approx. 8 minutes. Remove and run under cold water. On medium heat add oil, butter and garlic to a non-stick frying pan and sauté until garlic just begins to toast (be careful not to burn it). Add broccoli and turn gently until well coated and warm.

Note: 'Aioli' means garlic in Italian and traditionally means a rich sauce of crushed garlic, egg yolks, lemon juice and olive oil and some tend to use parsley and cherval.

Asparagus with Butter & Parmesan

SERVES 4

- *2 bunches asparagus*
- *1 tbs. (15g) butter, melted*
- *50g parmesan cheese, shaved*

Bring water to boil in a large frying pan, add asparagus and bring to the boil and then drain. Serve drizzled with melted butter and cheese. Season with sea salt and pepper.

Baked Onions

SERVES 4

- *4 onions — onion per person*
- *1 tbs. (15ml) olive oil*
- *½ cup (125ml) GF vegetable stock*

Preheat oven to 150°C. Cut the ends off the onions but do not peel them. Place them in a roasting tray and brush with oil. Pour the stock into the tray then bake for 1½ hours or until they are soft when gently squeezed. Place onions on serving dish and gently run a knife blade across the top in both directions to cut a cross. Peel back the skins and sprinkle black pepper on the tops. Serve.

Baked Rice

SERVES 4

- 1 cup (185g) rice, uncooked
- 2 tbs. (30g) butter, melted
- 2 cups (500ml) GF beef stock
- 50g parmesan cheese, grated

Preheat oven to 180°C. Place butter in a casserole dish, add rice and pour beef stock over it. Sprinkle with parmesan and bake for 45 minutes.

Beans & Pine Nuts

SERVES 4

These are scrumptious!

- 125g beans
- 3 tbs. (45ml) olive oil
- 4 tbs. pine nuts

Trim the beans, microwave for 1 minute then drain. Heat oil in a small non-stick frying pan over low heat. Add beans, sauté for a minute then add pine nuts, stir until heated through and pine nuts are lightly toasted.

Butter Bean & Potato Puree

SERVES 4

- *200g potatoes, peeled*
- *400g can butter beans*
- *1 tbs. (15ml) olive oil*
- *¼ cup (60ml) single cream*

Cook potatoes and beans until soft. Drain and mash to a puree, add oil and cream and stir until creamy and smooth.

Fried Brussels Sprouts

SERVES 4

- *12 Brussels sprouts*
- *4 rashers bacon*
- *1 tbs. walnut oil*
- *2 tbs. chopped walnuts*

Cut a criss-cross into the base of the sprouts. Boil approximately 8 minutes until cooked. Dice bacon and then fry until crisp, fold through the cooked sprouts with walnut oil and sauté for 2 minutes. Sprinkle with walnuts and serve.

Optional: Brussels sprouts can be substituted with cauliflower!

Fried Rice

SERVES 2 S.C.R.U.M.P.T.I.O.U.S!

- *1 cup (185g) brown rice*
- *1 egg*
- *2 rashers bacon*
- *4 tbs. (60ml) GF soy sauce*

While rice is boiling, fry the egg, breaking the yolk to ensure it spreads. Dice bacon and fry until crisp. Drain rice and rinse under hot water, stirring it to separate. Drain thoroughly and add to bacon and egg, cover evenly with soy sauce.

Optional: Also nice with diced pepper, pineapple, peas, chopped spring onions and corn and a tsp. of GF sweet chilli sauce.

Fluffy Rice Without a Cooker

SERVES 4–6

Recipe from Cyndi O'Meara.

- *5 cups (1.25 ltr.) boiling water*
- *2½ cups (460g) of long grain white rice, washed*

Preheat oven to 190°C. Place rice in a large glass ovenproof casserole dish with a lid. Add boiling water and stir until smooth. Cover and cook in oven for 30 minutes.

Garlic Mushrooms

SERVES 4

- *500g button mushrooms*
- *2 tbs. (30ml) olive oil*
- *1 or 2 cloves garlic, crushed*
- *6 stems flat-leaf parsley, chopped*

Preheat oven 180°C. Place mushrooms in a large baking dish, drizzle with oil and garlic, roast for 15 minutes or until mushrooms are tender and lightly browned. Stir in parsley.

Tip: Cook close to serving.

Herbed Courgettes

SERVES 4

- *3 courgettes, cut into thick diagonal slices*
- *1 tbs. (15g) butter*
- *1 tbs. finely chopped parsley*

Boil courgettes for 3 minutes in salted water then drain well. Heat butter in saucepan, add courgettes and season well. Sauté over low heat stirring occasionally until courgettes are golden brown. Sprinkle with chopped parsley.

Honey & Mustard Roast Parsnips

SERVES 6

- 1 kg parsnips, quartered
- 4 tbs. (60ml) olive oil
- 3 tbs. honey
- 4 tbs. GF wholegrain mustard

Preheat oven to 200°C. Bring the parsnips to the boil in lightly salted water and simmer for 5 minutes. Heat the oil in a large roasting tray. Drain the parsnips and add to the oil. Coat well and roast for 30 minutes until crispy. Mix the honey and mustard and pour over the parsnips, then cook for a further 5 minutes.

Honey Sesame Carrots

SERVES 4

- 6 carrots, peeled and cut in half lengthways
- 1 tbs. (15g) butter
- 1 tbs. honey
- 2 tbs. sesame seeds

In a saucepan bring water to boil, add carrots and boil for 4–5 minutes or until carrots are just tender. Drain, return to heat and add butter and honey and sauté. Add sesame seeds just as the carrots are starting to brown.

Peas with Mint & Garlic Butter

SERVES 4–6

- 1 kg pkt frozen peas
- 1 tbs. (15g) butter
- 1 clove garlic, crushed
- 6 stems fresh mint leaves, chopped

Cook the peas, drain and return to pan, add butter and garlic and season with sea salt and pepper. Gently toss before serving sprinkled with fresh mint leaves.

Roast Beetroot

SERVES 4

- 4 beetroot, quartered
- ¼ cup (60ml) olive oil
- ¼ cup (60ml) balsamic vinegar
- 6 stems fresh basil

Preheat oven 180°C. Mix together oil, vinegar and basil leaves. Place beetroot wedges into a baking dish and drizzle with the liquid. Roast for 30–35 minutes or until tender.

Roasted Corn with Parmesan & Cayenne

SERVES 4

- 4 fresh cobs of corn
- 2 tbs. GF mayonnaise
- 2 tbs. grated parmesan
- ½ tsp. cayenne pepper

Preheat oven 180°C. Place the corn, in its husks, directly on the oven rack and roast for 20 minutes until the corn is soft when you press on it. To finish, peel the husks, remove the corn silk, and tie the husks in a knot so you can hold on to it like a handle. Char the corn on a hot grill, or under a grill, until the kernels are slightly blackened all around and start popping (about 6 minutes). Rub the corn with mayonnaise, sprinkle with parmesan and cayenne pepper, ensure well coated.

Optional: Serve with lime wedges.

Sautéed Cherry Tomatoes

SERVES 4–6

- 2 tbs. (30g) butter
- 250g cherry tomatoes
- 2 tbs. fresh thyme leaves

Melt butter in a non-stick frying pan over medium heat. Add tomatoes and thyme and season generously. Cook for 5 minutes or until the tomatoes begin to soften.

Spicy Pumpkin Wedges

SERVES 4–6

- *400g pumpkin, peeled and cut into 4 wedges*
- *2 tbs. (30ml) olive oil*
- *1 tsp. ground cumin*
- *1 tsp. nutmeg*

Preheat oven to 180°C. Place pumpkin in a bowl, drizzle with oil and sprinkle with spices. Season with sea salt and pepper and toss to coat. Place on a baking tray and bake for 30 minutes or until tender, turning half way through cooking.

Spinach with Lemon

MAKES 4

This is a really nice way to eat spinach!

- *1 bunch fresh spinach, washed and shredded*
- *2 tbs. (30g) butter, softened*
- *2 tbs. (30ml) lemon juice*

Place spinach in saucepan of boiling water and boil for 5 minutes or until spinach has wilted. Drain well and return to dry saucepan, season with sea salt and pepper. Add butter and juice and toss together.

Optional: Another delicious way to eat spinach is to sprinkle it with GF mint sauce.

Stumpot

SERVES 2

Recipe from the lovely Lani Smith … A Dutch classic.

- *2 potatoes*
- *2 carrots*
- *1 large brown onion*
- *2 cups (500ml) GF stock (chicken or vegetable)*

Peel and chop first 3 ingredients. Place into a large saucepan with stock and season with pepper. Bring to the boil, reduce heat and simmer for 6–8 minutes or until vegetables are soft. Drain excess liquid and mash.

Vegie Kebabs

MAKES 16

The word 'kebab' is Arabic and means 'on a skewer'!

- *1 red pepper*
- *1 Spanish onion*
- *¼ fresh pineapple*
- *8 large mushrooms, washed and halved*

Cut first 3 ingredients into large chunks and thread alternately with mushrooms onto a soaked skewer. Grill on a hot BBQ for a couple of minutes each side or until soft and warm.

Mains

Those that know, do. Those that understand, teach.

Aristotle

Beef

Beef Stir-Fry

SERVES 4

- *500g stir fry beef*
- *⅔ cup (185g) GF BBQ sauce*
- *2 tbs. (30ml) sesame oil*
- *4–6 spring onions, chopped*

Mix stir-fry sauce and meat together; allow meat to stand for 15 minutes. Heat oil in a wok or frying pan. Stir-fry meat in batches for 1 minute, or until cooked on the outside and medium on the inside. Trim the spring onions and cut into thin lengthwise strips. Quickly stir-fry in wok. Serve meat on top of a salad (even just shredded ice-berg lettuce is nice) and top with spring onions and jus.

Tip: *How to Cook Stir-Fries:*

Chop ingredients into equal sizes so they will cook evenly.

Marinate meat for at least 2 hours for flavours to develop. But if you don't have time, even 15 minutes will improve the taste.

Make sure any oil used is very hot before adding ingredients.

Add vegies that take longer to cook first (carrots, onions); after 2 minutes add the other vegies (mange tout, pepper).

Add leafy greens and herbs to an almost completed stir-fry.

Beef Stew

SERVES 4

- 500g lean mince
- 1 large brown onion, chopped
- 120g cabbage, shredded
- 400g can GF tomato soup

Preheat oven to 180°C. Brown mince and onion in a non-stick frying pan. Drain and season with sea salt and pepper. Spread over the base of a casserole dish. Top with cabbage. Pour tomato soup on top and cover. Bake for 1 hour.

Beef Stroganoff

SERVES 4

Recipe from Glen Turnbull.

- 500g beef strips
- 1 pkt GF beef stroganoff seasoning
- 250g mushrooms, sliced
- 125g cream cheese, softened

Heat a non-stick frying pan and lightly fry beef strips. Add stroganoff mix with ½ cup of water and simmer until tender. Add cream cheese and stir until diluted. Add mushrooms and simmer for a further 5 minutes or until mushrooms soften.

Hint: Don't cook meat as it comes straight from the refrigerator. It will be far more tender if restored to room temperature first.

Coffee & Pepper Crusted Steaks

SERVES 4

This is charmingly unusual!

- *4 steaks, 2–3 cm thick*
- *2 tbs. whole coffee beans*
- *2 tbs. whole black peppercorns*
- *Olive oil spray*

Coarsely grind the coffee beans and peppercorns. Press the mixture evenly on both sides of the steaks. Spray steaks lightly with oil, then grill or barbecue the steaks over direct high heat for 8 to 10 minutes; turning once halfway through grilling time (do not turn steaks until you see beads of juice on the surface). Remove the steaks from the grill and season both sides with sea salt. Allow to rest for 3 minutes before serving.

Note: Have you ever wondered how long you should cook your steak for?

Try these cooking times advised by Chef Peter Wolf from the Eumundi Markets.

Well done: *5 minutes each side*

Medium: *3 minutes each side*

Rare: *2 minutes each side*

Based on a 2½ cm thick steak, cooked on a barbecue or hot grill.

Corned Beef

SERVES 6

- 1 kg corned beef
- 10 cloves
- ⅓ cup (80g) pure maple syrup
- Black pepper

Preheat oven to 180°C. Place meat in a large pot, cover with water. Bring to boil, reduce heat and cook for 1 hour or until tender. When cooked, place meat in a shallow baking dish, press cloves into meat, drizzle with syrup and dust with freshly cracked pepper. Place in the oven for 15 minutes.

Harch Steak

SERVES 2

Recipe by Karen Harch.

- 2 steaks of choice (eye fillet, rib fillet or lamb forequarters all work well)
- 3 tbs. tomato sauce
- 3 tbs. GF BBQ sauce
- 1 tbs. GF Worcestershire sauce

Preheat oven to 190°C. Mix all liquid ingredients together. Place meat in a casserole dish and pour over the meat. Cover and cook for 1 hour (or until meat is tender).

Massaman Curry

SERVES 4 Y.U.M.M.Y!!!

- *500g lean beef strips*
- *1 tbs. GF massaman curry paste*
- *3 desiree potatoes, peeled and cubed*
- *400ml coconut cream*

Place beef with 2 tbs. of water in a non-stick frying pan or large saucepan and cook on high heat till browned on the outside. Combine massaman curry and coconut cream and add to beef. Add potatoes and turn down to very lowest heat and simmer for 30 minutes or until potatoes are cooked through.

Optional: Can add ½ cup cashews and serve with rice.

Mustard Roast Beef

SERVES 4

The first roast Rach ever cooked! This tastes absolutely incredible and is a delicious winter's evening meal!

- *1 kg prime roasting beef*
- *4 tbs. GF grain mustard*
- *3 tbs. olive oil*

Preheat oven to 130°C. Place beef in a roasting pan and glaze generously with mustard. Drizzle with oil and bake for 3 hours (cooking it for this time will ensure the beef is well done but still very tender!) Turn beef at half way mark. Serve with your favourite roast vegies and GF gravy.

Pesto Stuffed Steaks

SERVES 4 F.A.S.T & F.A.B.U.L.O.U.S

- *2 beef rib eye steaks (about 3 cm thick)*
- *¼ cup (65g) GF basil pesto*
- *3 tbs. grated parmesan cheese*
- *1 tbs. (15ml) olive oil*

Preheat heavy frying pan until the pan is hot. Cut into the side of each steak, forming a deep pocket (do not cut through). Mix pesto and cheese and spread into pockets. Press closed and drizzle with oil. Place steaks carefully in the pan and cook for 6–8 minutes for a medium steak, turn once when you see juices on the surface. When done to your liking, remove, cover and let stand for 5–10 minutes. Cut beef into thick strips to serve.

Quick Meatloaf

SERVES 4

- *500g premium mince*
- *3 free range eggs, lightly beaten*
- *¾ cup GF breadcrumbs*
- *¼ cup (65g) tomato paste — reserve a tablespoon of paste*

Preheat oven to 180°C. Mix all ingredients together and place in a lined rectangular baking dish. Spread reserved tomato paste on top of meatloaf. Bake for 50 minutes or until lightly browned on top. Serve hot with vegetables, salad or mashed potato. This is also great to freeze.

Tip: For a Mexican meatloaf substitute tomato paste with a 270g jar of GF picante (hot) sauce. Use ⅔ of the sauce in the loaf and ⅓ to coat. Reduce eggs to 2.

Rissoles

MAKES 8

From playgroup chef extraordinaire, Aine Watkins!

- 500g premium mince
- 2 medium onions
- 2 medium free range eggs
- 1 tbs. GF plain flour

Preheat a sandwich press machine. Mix all ingredients, except for flour. Divide into 8 even amounts and roll into balls, binding with a small amount of flour. Place in between the sandwich press plates and cook until done.

Shepherd's Pie

SERVES 6

A recipe inspired from the Gippsland Harvest Festival, Victoria.

- 500g lean mince
- ½ cup (160g) GF fruit chutney
- 6 potatoes, boiled and mashed
- ¾ cup (75g) cheddar cheese, grated

Preheat oven to 180°C. In a non-stick frying pan brown mince, season and mix through chutney. Pour into a casserole dish, top with even layer of mashed potato and sprinkle with grated cheese. Bake for 20–30 minutes or until cheese is nice and bubbly.

Optional: Slice a tomato or two over the mince before topping with potato.

Soy Steak

Recipe by Brian Boholt.

- 4 scotch fillet steaks
- 4 tbs. GF soy sauce
- 1 tbs. brown sugar
- 1 clove garlic, crushed

Mix soy sauce, brown sugar and garlic together. Marinate steak in mixture for 3 hours. Grill or BBQ steak for 3–4 minutes on both sides or until done to your liking.

Optional: Serve with a crisp, fresh salad.

Steak Burgundy

SERVES 2

A recipe from Paul at the Buderim Butchers, QLD.

- 2 good sized rib fillet steaks
- 1 cup (250ml) red wine
- ½ tbs. butter
- 2 cloves garlic, crushed

Preheat oven to 180°C. Marinate steaks in red wine for 2 hours then place each steak in an envelope of aluminium foil ensuring you have plenty of foil to twist the top over to seal in steak later. Mix butter and garlic together and place an equal dollop of mixture on top of each steak. Seal the steak in by folding over foil. Put on a baking tray and bake in oven for 45 minutes. YUM. YUM. YUM!

Optional: Serve with roast vegetables or salad.

Steak with Mushroom Ragout

SERVES 4 AND IS DELICIOUS!

- *4 steaks*
- *2 tbs. (30g) butter*
- *100g mushrooms, sliced*
- *125ml double cream*

Brush steaks with half the butter. Preheat a non-stick frying pan to hot. Cook first sides until moisture appears (approx. 3–4 minutes), turn and cook for another 3–4 minutes for a steak cooked to 'medium'. Remove from oven, cover with aluminium foil and allow the steak to rest for 5 minutes. Meanwhile, place butter and mushrooms in the frying pan and cook until softened. Add cream and simmer until reduced and thickened (may need a little more cream). Season with sea salt and pepper.

Optional: Serve with boiled potatoes and green beans.

Veal with Olives

SERVES 4

- *4 veal cutlets, pounded paper thin*
- *¼ cup (55g) butter*
- *⅓ cup (80ml) Marsala wine*
- *10 green olives, sliced*

Sprinkle meat with sea salt and pepper. Simmer very quickly in melted butter, browning lightly on both sides. Add Marsala wine and olives and heat for one minute and serve with your choice of vegies.

Veal Steaks with Creamy Pepper Sauce

SERVES 4

- *4 veal steaks*
- *1 tbs. lemon pepper*
- *⅓ cup marinated peppers, drained and pureed*
- *¾ cup (180ml) double cream*

Grill steaks to your liking, cover with aluminium foil. Place remaining ingredients into a non-stick frying pan and simmer until it thickens. Serve sauce generously drizzled over veal.

Chicken

Creativity is allowing yourself to make mistakes.
Art is knowing which ones to keep.

Scott Adams

Apricot Glazed Chicken

SERVES 2

- 2 chicken breasts
- ⅓ cup (100g) apricot preserve
- 2 tsp. GF Dijon mustard
- 5 drops GF hot sauce

Preheat oven to 220°C. Rinse chicken with cold water and pat dry. Place in a baking dish. In a small bowl, mix the preserve, mustard and hot sauce. Spoon over chicken. Bake chicken for 15 minutes. Baste with sauce that drips from the chicken. Bake for a further 10 minutes.

Bacon Encrusted Chicken

MAKES 6

- 3 chicken breasts, halved
- 250g cream cheese with onions and chives
- 1 tbs. (15g) butter
- 6 bacon rashers, rindless

Preheat oven to 180°C. Tenderise chicken to 1 cm thickness. Spread 3 tbs. cream cheese over each. Dot with a little butter and season. Roll up and wrap each with a strip of bacon. Place seam side down onto a greased baking tray and bake for 20 minutes or until juices run clear.

Cheese & Ham Chicken Rolls

SERVES 2

- *2 chicken breast fillets*
- *2 pieces Swiss cheese*
- *2 pieces sliced ham off the bone*
- *1 tbs. GF grainy mustard*

Preheat oven to 180°C. Using a rolling pin, flatten chicken before smearing with mustard. Lay a piece of cheese followed by a piece of ham on each. Roll up and secure opening with a toothpick. Bake for 20 minutes or until brown and cooked through. Remove toothpick and cut into rounds to serve.

Chicken Marsala

SERVES 2

Sensational!

- *4 chicken breasts*
- *200g sliced fresh mushrooms*
- *½ cup (125ml) Marsala wine*
- *¾ cup (180ml) double cream*

Flatten chicken a little and cut into strips. Sauté chicken in a large non-stick frying pan for 15–20 minutes or until cooked through and juices run clear. Add mushrooms and sauté until soft. Add Marsala wine and bring to boil. Boil for 2–4 minutes, seasoning with sea salt and pepper to taste if you like. Stir in the cream and simmer until heated through, about 5 minutes.

Optional: Serve with vegetables.

Chicken, Pumpkin & Chickpea Curry

SERVES 6

In the words of Wendy Beattie 'This is fabulous!'

- *700g piece pumpkin*
- *6 boneless, skinless chicken thighs*
- *300g can chickpeas*
- *435g jar GF korma curry sauce*

De-seed pumpkin, and steam for 5–10 minutes or until almost cooked. Peel and cut into cubes. Cut chicken thighs in half. Drain chickpeas. Place chicken, pumpkin, chickpeas and curry sauce in a saucepan. Wash jar with about ¼ cup of hot water and add to saucepan. Cover and cook on medium for about 30 minutes.

Optional: Serve with steamed rice and garnish with fresh coriander. Replace water with coconut cream.

Chicken Tikka Masala

SERVES 4

You will cook this again and again and again!

- *3 chicken breasts, cut into chunks*
- *2 tbs. GF tikka masala paste*
- *400g can of GF tomato soup*
- *2–3 tbs. natural yoghurt*

Heat a non-stick frying pan, add the chicken and fry for 5–6 minutes or until browned. Add the curry paste and soup and simmer for 15 minutes, then stir in the yoghurt and heat through.

Optional: Serve with rice.

Chutney Chicken Dish

SERVES 2

This is deliciously simple!

- *2 chicken breasts*
- *2 tbs. GF fruit chutney*
- *2 tbs. GF French mustard*
- *30g cheddar cheese, grated*

Preheat oven to 180°C. Mix the chutney with the mustard and cover the chicken breasts. Put chicken breasts in a baking dish, cover with grated cheese and place in oven for 15–20 minutes.

Optional: Serve with rice or vegetables.

Green Chicken Curry

SERVES 4

A ripper recipe from Shane McCosker.

- *4 chicken thighs, boneless and skinless*
- *80g green beans, cut into 5 cm pieces*
- *¼ cup (65g) GF green curry paste*
- *400ml can coconut cream*

Cut chicken into strips. Heat your wok or large frying pan and add green curry paste, cooking and stirring for a minute or so or until fragrant. Add chicken and cook, stirring for about 10 minutes until almost done. Stir in coconut cream and bring to boil. Simmer uncovered for 30 minutes. Add beans and simmer for 10 minutes, or until just tender.

Optional: We often add more vegetables.

Indian Chicken Curry

MAKES 4

Very easy and very yummy!

- *1 roast chicken, remove skin*
- *225g natural yoghurt*
- *6 tbs. GF mayonnaise*
- *2 tbs. GF curry powder*

Preheat oven to 175°C. Chop roast chicken into bite sized pieces. In a bowl mix together yoghurt, mayo and curry powder. Marinate chicken pieces in yoghurt mixture for at least 1 hour then bake in a moderate oven until heated through.

Optional: Serve with rice, fresh coriander and lemon wedges.

Italian Chicken

SERVES 4

This is sooooooooooooooo good!!!

- *4 chicken breast fillets, sliced*
- *410g canned basil and onion tomatoes*
- *50g pitted kalamata olives*
- *100g grated cheese*

Preheat oven to 180°C. Arrange chicken on the base of a casserole dish. Mix tomatoes and olives together and pour over chicken. Sprinkle grated cheese over the top. Bake for 20 minutes or until chicken is tender.

Optional: Substitute tomatoes for your favourite GF pasta sauce.

Mango Chicken

SERVES 4

- ⅔ cup (210g) GF mango chutney
- 1 tbs. GF Dijon mustard
- ½ bunch fresh coriander, chopped
- 600g chicken breast fillets

Preheat oven 200°C. Combine first three ingredients in a bowl. Cut chicken into strips and coat well with chutney mix. Place on a paper lined baking tray and bake for 15–20 minutes or until cooked.

Optional: Serve with steamed rice and vegetables and garnish with fresh coriander.

Soy Chicken

SERVES 4–6

- 1 kg chicken pieces
- ½ cup (110g) light brown sugar
- ½ cup (125ml) GF soy sauce
- 1 tbs. (15g) butter

Preheat oven to 180°C. Place chicken skin side down into a baking dish. Combine remaining ingredients in small saucepan and place over low heat until butter is melted. Stir well to mix then pour over chicken. Bake for 20 minutes, turn and bake for another 20 minutes, basting occasionally.

Sweet & Spicy Chicken

SERVES 2

- 6 chicken legs
- ½ cup (160g) orange marmalade
- 1–2 tsp. GF chilli powder

Preheat oven to 180°C. Combine marmalade and chilli powder in a plastic sandwich bag, add chicken legs and shake until evenly coated. Place chicken on aluminium foil on a baking tray and spoon on any remaining marmalade/chilli powder. Bake for 30 minutes or until done.

Tangy Chicken Tenderloins

SERVES 4

- 3 chicken breasts, sliced
- 3 tbs. GF plain flour
- 1 cup (280g) GF BBQ sauce
- ½ cup (125ml) orange juice

Preheat oven to 180°C. Coat chicken with GF flour. Brown in a non-stick pan and place in a shallow baking pan. Mix BBQ sauce and juice and pour over chicken. Bake covered in oven for 15 minutes. Remove from oven, spoon sauce over chicken and bake uncovered for another 5 minutes.

Thai Chicken with Cucumber Noodles

SERVES 4

Recipe by Dan Primmer. This is just so tasty!

- *2 chicken breasts, cut into chunky pieces*
- *½ cup (160g) GF sweet chilli and ginger sauce*
- *1 continental cucumber*
- *½ cup crunchy GF rice noodles*

Place chicken in a non-stick frying pan with ¼ cup water and cook till water evaporates. Add sauce and simmer for 5 minutes or until the chicken is cooked through. Remove from heat. Slice and julienne cucumber to resemble long, thin noodles. Add cucumber and noodles to chicken and mix gently. Serve topped with extra cucumber noodles as garnish.

Wings with Curry Honey Glaze

Makes a lot! A recipe from the charming Kimmy Morrison.

- *2 kg chicken wings*
- *¼ cup (80g) honey*
- *2 tsp. GF curry powder*
- *2 tsp. GF soy sauce*

Combine honey, curry powder and soy sauce and marinate with chicken overnight in the fridge in an air-tight container. BBQ wings until cooked through. Baste frequently during cooking process.

Fish & Seafood

Only Robinson Crusoe had everything done by Friday!!!

A Parent

Baked Fish

SERVES 2

- *2 fresh white fish fillets*
- *1 tsp. butter*
- *1 lemon*

Preheat oven to 180°C. Coat fish with melted butter and season with sea salt and pepper. Cut lemon and put slices on fish. Wrap fish in aluminium foil. Cook in oven for 20 minutes or until fish is tender.

Baked Salmon with Pesto Crust

SERVES 4

A recipe from Michelle Dodd. *THIS IS FANTASTIC!*

- *4 salmon steaks*
- *4 tbs.GF basil pesto*
- *50g pecorino cheese, finely grated*
- *1 lemon*

Preheat oven to 175°C. Sear salmon steaks on each side for 2 minutes, skin side down first. Meanwhile combine pesto and cheese. Spread this mixture over salmon steaks and squeeze fresh lemon juice over the top. Bake in oven for 15 minutes.

Cheesy Fish Steaks

SERVES 4

- 4 fish steaks
- ¾ cup (75g) grated cheese
- 1 tsp. GF Worcestershire sauce
- 1 tbs. (15ml) milk

Place fish steaks under a 160°C grill for 5 minutes. Mix remaining ingredients and season with sea salt and pepper. Turn the fish and spread the uncooked side with cheese mix. Grill for a further 5 minutes or until fish is cooked and the topping bubbling.

Optional: Garnish with chopped fresh parsley.

Curried Fish with Coconut Rice

SERVES 4

This is a great way to make rice for a change!

- 4 fresh white fish fillets
- 283g jar GF korma curry sauce
- 400g can coconut milk
- 1 cup (185g) jasmine rice

Cut fish into 2 cm cubes. Place in a saucepan with curry sauce. Bring to the boil and simmer for 5 minutes or until fish is cooked. Bring ½ cup (125ml) water and coconut milk to the boil. Add rice and cook for 12–15 minutes or until rice is tender and liquid absorbed. Pile rice onto four individual serving plates. Top with fish mixture.

Optional: Garnish with fresh coriander.

Dukkah Crusted Salmon

SERVES 4

- 4 skinless salmon fillets
- Olive oil spray
- ⅓ cup dukkah

Preheat oven to 150°C. Place salmon on a lined baking tray. Lightly spray each fillet with oil, then press dukkah onto both sides of each salmon fillet. Bake for 15 minutes.

Fish with Lemon Butter

SERVES 4

- 4 fish fillets
- 1 tbs. (15g) butter
- 1 lemon, juiced
- 3 stems fresh parsley, chopped

Season fish with pepper. Place under grill. Mix butter, juice and ½ tsp. rind together and spread over fish. Grill until lightly browned. Turn carefully then spread with remaining lemon mix. Grill until cooked. Serve garnished with lemon slices and parsley.

Hint: Often a nice accompaniment to fish is a glass of water with ice cubes that have been frozen with little slices of lemon in them.

Fish with Mango & Kiwifruit

SERVES 2

- *4 fresh white fish fillets*
- *1 tbs. (15g) butter*
- *2 kiwifruit*
- *1 mango*

Brush fish with melted butter and on a hot grill or BBQ, grill each side for 3–5 minutes, depending on thickness. Peel and slice the kiwifruit and mango and sauté lightly in the remaining butter. Serve layered on top of fish.

Garlic Cream King Prawns

SERVES 4

A simple classic from Aine Watkins that will make a chef of anyone!

- *1½ cups (270g) rice*
- *16 raw king or tiger prawns, peeled and de-veined*
- *125ml double cream*
- *2 cloves garlic, crushed*

Boil rice, then rinse under hot water. Meanwhile, place garlic and cream in a wok or non-stick frying pan and reduce. Add prawns and cook until orange in colour and warmed through. Serve on a bed of rice.

Herb Crusted Fish

SERVES 4

- 4 white fish fillets
- ½ cup (65g) GF breadcrumbs
- 3 stems fresh flat-leaf parsley, chopped
- 50g parmesan cheese, grated

Preheat oven 200°C. Place fish on an aluminium foil-lined baking tray. Combine remaining ingredients and season with sea salt and black pepper. Sprinkle over fish and bake in oven for 15–20 minutes or until cooked.

Optional: Delicious served with lemon potatoes and a green salad.

Lime & Salmon Cakes

SERVES 6

A recipe from Jennette McCosker ... Y.u.m.m.y!

- 1 lime
- 415g can pink salmon, drained
- 1 free range egg
- 3 slices GF bread, grated into crumbs

Grate lime zest and then juice. In a bowl, tip zest, juice and remaining ingredients, season with sea salt and pepper. Mix well before shaping into 12 thick cakes. Cook in a non-stick pan until heated through.

Hint: Fresh GF bread is easier to grate when frozen.

Oregano Fish

SERVES 4

Recipe by Sue Edmonstone.

- 4 white fish fillets
- 2 tbs. (30ml) olive oil
- ½ bunch fresh oregano, leaves only
- 2 cloves garlic, crushed

Coat fish with oil then sprinkle the oregano and cracked pepper over both sides of the fillets. Place fish into a non-stick frying pan over medium to high heat. Sprinkle garlic over the top and cook for about 1–2 minutes or until golden then flip and cook for a further 2 minutes. Serve with salad.

Salmon Delight

SERVES 4

A recipe from the radiant Katrina Price.

- 4 salmon steaks, skinless
- 4 slices prosciutto
- 200g green beans, top 'n' tailed
- 12 cherry tomatoes

Preheat oven to 180°C. Wrap the salmon steaks in prosciutto and place in a baking dish. Add the cherry tomatoes and beans. Bake for 10–15 minutes.

Optional: For a special occasion top with some toasted pine nuts and a drizzle of lemon juice.

Salmon Roulade

SERVES 4

Recipe by Chef Dan Primmer.

- *4 x 200g salmon steaks*
- *200g Danish feta, sliced into rectangular strips*
- *200g semi-dried tomatoes*
- *80g baby spinach*

Preheat oven to 180°C. Cut a 40 cm long piece of aluminium foil and lay it flat, place same length of grease-proof paper on top. Butterfly salmon (cut in half without cutting all the way through) and place in the middle of the aluminium foil. In a bowl, combine remaining ingredients and spread lengthways along the salmon. Roll salmon into a tight roll, twisting the ends to secure the contents. Place on a baking tray and bake for 15–20 minutes in oven. Slice into desired portions.

Optional: Serve with a Butter Bean & Potato Puree (see Vegetables) or a Rocket & Parmesan Salad (see Salads).

Salmon with Honey & Mint

SERVES 4

- *4 salmon steaks*
- *1 tbs. honey*
- *1 tbs. freshly chopped mint*
- *1 lime*

In a shallow dish, combine honey, mint and the juice from half the lime and season with sea salt and pepper. Add the salmon and marinate for 10–15 minutes. Preheat the grill to a high heat. Lift salmon from marinade, allowing excess to drip off. Grill for approximately 5–8 minutes depending on thickness of salmon. Serve garnished with remaining lime.

Snapper & Almond Crust

SERVES 4

A recipe from Michelle Dodd to delight even the fussiest fish eaters.

- *50g parmesan cheese, finely grated*
- *1 cup (170g) almond meal*
- *2 free range eggs*
- *4 medium snapper fillets*

Preheat oven to 220°C. Combine cheese and almond meal in a shallow medium bowl. Beat eggs in a second shallow bowl. Dip fish fillets, one at a time, in egg then almond mixture to coat both sides. Place fish in a single layer on an oven tray covered with non-stick baking paper. Cook fish uncovered for about 20 minutes or until cooked to your liking.

Hint: Cut into small fingers for 'fish fingers with a twist' that kids will love!

Sunshine Prawns

SERVES 4

A recipe from Dan Primmer ... One word — FABALICIOUS!

- *400g can coconut cream*
- *20 uncooked prawns, peeled and deveined*
- *½ fresh pineapple, diced*
- *2 large chillis, chopped*

Pour cream into a non-stick frying pan and bring to boil over medium heat. Reduce heat, add remaining ingredients and simmer until warmed through and prawns turn orange. Delicious served over steamed rice.

Swiss Fish

SERVES 4

- 4 fillets of cleaned and boned sea perch, dory or large whiting
- 1 ripe avocado
- 2 tbs. (30g) butter
- 4 slices Swiss cheese

Preheat oven to 180°C. Melt butter in a non-stick frying pan on medium heat. Add fish fillets, cooking on 1 side for approx. 2 minutes before flipping (cooking time is dependent on how thick the fish fillet is). Lay cooked fillets on a tray lined with baking paper and top with Swiss cheese. Melt in oven for about 5 minutes and then top with a sliver or two of avocado and serve with salad.

Tandoori Salmon

SERVES 4

- 4 salmon fillets
- 2 tbs. (30ml) olive oil
- 2 tbs. GF tandoori paste
- 80g natural yoghurt

Preheat oven to 200°C. Line a baking tray with baking paper. Rub oil over the salmon fillets and season with sea salt. Brush with paste. Heat remaining oil in a large non-stick frying pan over high heat. Add salmon, skin side down and cook for 2 minutes. Turn and cook until golden. Transfer to the lined tray and bake for 8 minutes for medium or until cooked to your liking. Dollop with yoghurt before serving.

Optional: Serve over a bed of salad drizzled with lime juice and fresh coriander.

Tuna & Tomato Risotto

SERVES 4

A recipe from the talented Marie McColl.

- *425g can flaked tuna in brine, drained*
- *410g can chopped tomatoes*
- *2 cups (370g) arborio rice*
- *5 cups (1.25ltr.) GF vegetable stock*

Bring stock to boil, add rice and reduce heat and simmer for 20 minutes. Add tuna and tomatoes, season with sea salt and pepper. Continue to simmer until all liquid has absorbed, stirring regularly, and then serve.

Tony's Delicious Quick Mango Fish

SERVES 4

Recipe from our favourite 'barbecuer' Tony Van Dijk.

- *4 pieces of fresh, boned and cleaned swordfish/mahi mahi or marlin*
- *¼ cup (60ml) olive oil*
- *Cracked pepper*
- *2 fresh mangoes*

Coat fish liberally with oil and pepper. Cook on a medium heated BBQ surface or flat non-stick frying pan. Cook fish till you can see the flesh turning white up to half way through, and then grind some more cracked pepper onto the exposed non-cooked surface before flipping over. Serve with BBQ or pan-cooked fresh mango flesh.

Lamb

From what we get, we can make a living.
But from what we give, makes a life.

Arthur Ashe

Bocconcini Lamb Steaks

SERVES 4

- *4 medium sized lamb steaks*
- *4 pieces roasted red peppers*
- *2 tbs. (30ml) lemon juice*
- *6 pieces fresh bocconcini, sliced*

Using a meat mallet, gently pound the lamb steaks. Cook in a non-stick pan until lightly browned. Place steaks onto a non-stick baking tray. Combine peppers and juice in a small bowl and divide mixture over each steak and top with sliced bocconcini. Grill for about 5 minutes or until cheese melts and topping is nice and warm.

Chinese-Style Lamb Roast

SERVES 4–6

Try it … You'll be surprised!

- *1½ kg lamb roast*
- *375ml can evaporated milk*
- *½ cup (160g) GF hoi sin or GF teriyaki sauce*

Preheat oven to 180°C. Place the lamb into an oven bag. Combine the milk and sauce. Pour about half over the lamb (remaining can be frozen for another time) and tightly seal the bag, piercing a few holes around the end. Roast the lamb for 1 hour and 45 minutes or until cooked as desired. Serve with fried rice.

Optional: Garnish with fresh coriander.

Glazed Lamb Chops

SERVES 4–6

- *4 to 6 lamb loin chops, about 2 cm thick*
- *⅓ cup (100g) orange marmalade*
- *2 tbs. (30ml) lemon juice*

Place lamb under a grill for 6 minutes, season with sea salt and pepper and turn. Grill the other side for 5 minutes or until almost cooked. Season second side. Combine the marmalade and lemon juice and spread evenly over lamb. Grill for about 2 minutes longer.

Lamb Chops with Roast Pepper Mayonnaise

SERVES 4

- *1 cup (80g) roasted peppers*
- *½ cup (130g) GF whole egg mayonnaise*
- *8 lamb mid-loin chops*

Cook lamb on a heated non-stick grill or BBQ plate. Blend pepper and mayonnaise until smooth. Serve chops with a dollop of pepper mayonnaise.

Lamb Cutlets Kilpatrick

SERVES 4

These are really scrummy! Morgan is 7 and asks for these EVERY week!!!

- *16 lamb cutlets*
- *½ cup (160g) GF spicy red sauce (may need a little more)*
- *6 bacon rashers, chopped and lightly fried*

Grill chops until cooked through. Place on a baking paper lined tray, and spread sauce evenly over each cutlet. Sprinkle with bacon and pop under a warm grill for a few minutes or until bacon is crispy.

Lamb Pesto Cutlets

SERVES 3

Everyone looooooooooooooves these!

- *6 lamb cutlets*
- *3 tbs. GF basil pesto*
- *3 tbs. parmesan cheese*

Preheat oven to 180°C. Place cutlets on a baking paper lined tray. Combine pesto and parmesan and dollop 1 tbs. of mixture on top of each cutlet. Place in the oven and cook for 20–30 minutes or until cooked through.

Note: Paul does this one by cooking it on the BBQ — cook one side of the cutlets first before turning over and then placing the pesto and parmesan mixture on top of the cooked side, continue to cook to your liking.

Lamb, Rosemary & Chorizo Skewers

MAKES 12

- *4 lamb loins*
- *2 GF chorizo sausages, cut into thick slices*
- *4 sprigs fresh rosemary*
- *⅓ cup (80ml) olive oil*

Preheat oven 200°C. Cut lamb into pieces (you want approx. 24) place in a bowl with chorizo, rosemary and oil. Marinate for 30 minutes. Thread one piece of lamb with a slice of chorizo twice, then place the skewers on a paper lined baking tray. Bake for 10 minutes.

Quick Lamb Rogan Josh

SERVES 4

- *500g diced lamb*
- *250g Greek yoghurt*
- *4 tbs. GF garam marsala*
- *2 x 400g cans GF tomato, onion and herb mix*

Marinate lamb in fridge for 3 hours with yoghurt and garam marsala. In a large pot over medium heat, add ½ cup of water then lamb, bring to a simmer, add tomatoes and simmer on low heat for 2½ hours. If required add more water.

Roast Lamb

MAKES 4–6

A recipe by the lovely Jan Neale — one the Turnbull family love to be invited to on a Sunday night.

- *1 kg leg of lamb (or shoulder)*
- *1 sprig rosemary*
- *2 cloves garlic, sliced*
- *2 tbs. (30ml) olive oil*

Preheat oven to 200°C. Cut a 2 cm slit across the lamb in several places and insert 6 rosemary leaves and a slice of garlic. Coat the baking dish with oil and bake for about 1 hour. Serve with roast vegetables and GF gravy.

Tangy Lamb Balls

SERVES 4

A fabulous recipe that is definitely worth trying from Perditta O'Connor.

- *500g lamb mince*
- *1 tsp. GF curry powder*
- *3 tbs. (45g) GF sweet chilli sauce*
- *Juice of 1 lemon*

Place all ingredients into a large bowl and combine. Roll into patties and fry in a non-stick frying pan until crunchy on the outside (this means it is cooked well on the inside).

Optional: Add a clove of garlic to the mixture. Serve with jasmine rice and a mint yoghurt dipping sauce. Roll into small balls and serve with GF sweet chilli sauce as a nibble on their own.

Teriyaki Lamb Skewers

SERVES 4

- *2 tbs. (30ml) GF Tamari soy sauce*
- *2 tbs. (30ml) mirin*
- *1 tsp. caster sugar*
- *600g diced lamb*

Combine all ingredients in a bowl. Allow flavours to develop for approx. 30 minutes. Thread lamb onto bamboo skewers that have been soaking in cold water. Grill or BBQ.

Pasta

Fun is about as good a habit as there is …

Jimmy Buffet

Alfredo

SERVES 4

This is simply sensational!

- ¼ cup (55g) butter
- 250ml double cream
- 100g parmesan cheese, shaved
- 200g fresh GF fettuccine

While boiling pasta, melt butter in a large pan and add cream bringing it to the boil. Simmer for 5 minutes, stirring constantly, add ¾ of the parmesan cheese and season well. Reduce heat, add drained (not rinsed) pasta and toss until thoroughly coated. Serve sprinkled with remaining parmesan.

Beef & Pumpkin Pasta

SERVES 4

- *500g extra lean beef mince*
- *500ml GF tomato pasta sauce*
- *300g pumpkin, peeled and cubed*
- *240g GF spiral pasta*

Brown mince in a large non-stick frying pan. Add pasta sauce and bring to boil. Reduce heat and simmer for 20 minutes. Steam pumpkin until tender and fold into beef mixture. While sauce is cooking, cook pasta in boiling water. Drain and serve among four plates. Top with beef and pumpkin sauce.

Blue Broccoli Penne Pasta

SERVES 4

- *400g pkt GF penne pasta*
- *1 large head broccoli, cut into florets*
- *125g blue cheese*
- *250g tub sour cream*

Add pasta to a saucepan of boiling water. Cook for 8 minutes (or according to manufacturer's instructions), then drain. Similarly, add broccoli to a saucepan of boiling water, boil for 4 minutes or until just cooked through. Drain. Meanwhile add blue cheese and sour cream to a non-stick frying pan over low heat and reduce to a thick, creamy sauce. Toss through broccoli and pasta, heat through and serve warm.

Optional: Serve topped with toasted pine nuts.

Florentine Carbonara

SERVES 4

Recipe from Julie Stephens. *THIS IS TIMELESS!!*

- *350g pkt GF spaghetti*
- *5 rashers rindless bacon, diced*
- *2 free range eggs, lightly beaten*
- *100g parmesan cheese, shaved*

Bring a medium saucepan of water to the boil. Add the spaghetti and boil according to manufacturer's instructions. While spaghetti is boiling, lightly fry bacon strips in a non-stick frying pan. Once spaghetti is cooked, drain (do not rinse) and add beaten eggs immediately, stirring through hot pasta. Add bacon and cheese and toss to combine. Serve immediately.

Optional: Fry bacon with a little garlic.

Gnocchi

MAKES APPROX. 30 AND IS FABULOUS!

- *1½ cups (275g) GF plain flour*
- *250g tub ricotta*
- *1 egg yolk*

In a bowl, sift flour. Add ricotta and egg yolk. With hands, mix into a dough making sure it is smooth and not sticking to the sides (if mixture is wet, add a little more flour). Roll into 2 cm balls and with a fork press gnocchi and roll it towards yourself. Set aside and cover to prevent drying. Bring a pot of salted water to boil, add gnocchi and when it floats remove and drain.

Tip: To get best flavour, pan fry with butter until light golden brown.

Homemade Napolitana Sauce

SERVES 4

- *400g can tomatoes*
- *2 tbs. (30ml) olive oil*
- *2 cloves garlic, crushed*
- *½ bunch fresh basil, leaves only*

Pour oil into a non-stick frying pan over medium heat and add garlic. Sauté, stirring for 30 seconds. Add tomatoes. Season with sea salt and pepper and simmer over low heat for 10 minutes. Stir in basil and allow to simmer for 5 more minutes.

Macaroni Bake

SERVES 4. A recipe from the wonderful Jenny Postle.

- *2 cups cooked GF macaroni*
- *410g can thick and tasty tomato puree*
- *250g diced GF ham or bacon*
- *80g grated cheese*

Preheat oven to 180°C. Place macaroni, tomato puree, ham and half the grated cheese in a bowl and mix well before pouring into a casserole dish. Top with remaining grated cheese and bake for 20 minutes.

Optional: Mix some freshly grated GF breadcrumbs into the cheese topping.

Pasta with Tomato & Basil

SERVES 4. The kids will love this, too.

- *200g GF pasta*
- *500g GF tomato pasta sauce with herbs (sugo)*
- *½ bunch basil, leaves torn*
- *50g parmesan cheese, shaved*

Place pasta into a saucepan of boiling water and cook for about 6 minutes then drain. Place sugo into a non-stick saucepan and simmer. Add pasta to the simmering sugo and most of the parmesan. When the pasta is al dente, stir though the basil leaves and serve with parmesan and a basil leaf on top.

Hint: Basil leaves are best torn rather than chopped as their leaves don't bruise when torn.

Note: 'Sugo' means 'juice' in Italian, as well as sauce, and there are plenty available for purchase at most supermarkets.

Pepper Pesto Fettuccini

SERVES 4 ... and is so flavoursome!

- *220g GF fettuccini*
- *1 cup (250ml) double cream*
- *½ cup (130g) GF red pepper pesto*
- *4 tbs. chopped chives*

Cook pasta according to manufacturer's instructions (be careful NOT to over cook it). Drain, reserving ¼ cup cooking liquid. Return pasta to saucepan. Combine cream and pesto in a medium frying pan over low heat. Cook and stir for 5 minutes or until mixture comes to the boil. Add pasta, reserved cooking liquid and chives to cream sauce, season with sea salt and pepper and toss gently.

Optional: Sprinkle with extra chopped chives.

Pesto Pasta

SERVES 4

- *450g GF fettucine*
- *340g GF basil pesto*
- *2 cups (150g) cherry tomatoes, halved*
- *100g parmesan cheese, grated*

Cook pasta to manufacturer's instructions. Stir in basil pesto, tossing gently over low heat until pasta is coated. Add grape tomatoes and toss for 1 minute. Sprinkle with cheese and serve.

Pinenut Pasta

SERVES 2

Recipe by forever NSW loyal Lea 'Boof' Van Dijk

- *100g pkt GF fettucine*
- *70g pine nuts*
- *1 tbs. (15g) butter*
- *50g parmesan cheese, grated*

Put butter and pine nuts in a warm non-stick frying pan and cook until golden brown. Bring a saucepan of water to the boil and cook pasta to packet instructions. Drain water and toss pasta with pine nuts and parmesan.

Optional: A little cracked pepper tastes great too.

Sun-dried Pesto Pasta

SERVES 4

A recipe by Alistair Beattie that shocked us at its simplicity and taste!

- *350g tubular GF spaghetti*
- *4 rashers rindless bacon, diced*
- *80g pine nuts*
- *4 tbs. GF sun-dried tomato pesto*

While you are cooking pasta, fry bacon until brown. Toast pine nuts for 2–3 minutes in preheated 150°C oven. When spaghetti is ready, drain and rinse with boiling water. Mix with 4 tbs. of pesto and toss through bacon and pine nuts. Add more pesto, if desired.

What we learnt when cooking with gluten free pasta is to:

FOLLOW THE MANUFACTURER'S INSTRUCTIONS!

Over cooking gluten free pasta results in thick, gluggy pasta that your guests will tease you about all night!!!!

Pork

*I may not have gone where I intended to go
but I think I have ended up where I intended to be.*

Douglas Adams

Bacon & Cannellini Risotto

SERVES 4 AND IS S.C.R.U.M.P.T.I.O.U.S!

- 4 rashers of bacon, roughly chopped
- 5 cups (1.25ltr.) GF chicken stock
- 2 cups (370g) arborio rice
- 400g can cannellini beans

Fry bacon in large non-stick frying pan. Bring stock to boil in a saucepan. Add rice to frying pan with bacon and stir well, add stock, reduce heat, cover and simmer for 20 minutes. Add beans, season with sea salt and pepper. Continue to simmer until rice is soft and stock has been fully absorbed.

Optional: Replace cannellini beans with peas.

Country BBQ Pork Ribs

SERVES 4

- 2 kg pork ribs
- 2 large onions, sliced
- 1 clove garlic, crushed
- 375g bottle of your favourite GF BBQ sauce

Place ribs in bottom of slow cooker. Add onions, garlic, and GF BBQ sauce. Cover and cook on low for 7–8 hours.

Grilled Pork with Parmesan Polenta

SERVES 2

Recipe by the talented Matt Tebbutt when filming Market Kitchen in the UK.

- *4 pork chops*
- *4 cups (1ltr.) GF vegetable stock*
- *1 cup (160g) polenta*
- *75g parmesan cheese, finely grated*

Preheat oven to 190°C. Into a hot frying pan, place pork chops, season with sea salt and cook for 2–3 minutes (depending on thickness) before turning. Cook for another 2–3 minutes or until juices run clear. Remove and place on a baking tray and bake in oven for 5 minutes. Meanwhile, bring stock to the boil (start with 3 cups and add more if needed) then add polenta. This should not thicken, it takes on quite a wet consistency. Add the parmesan and season with sea salt and pepper to taste. Spoon polenta onto serving plate and place 2 chops on top of polenta, pour over juices from the baking tray and serve.

Note: If chops are quite large this may make 3–4 serves.

Tip: Chef Dan Primmer advised us to 'Treat your plate like a canvas and work from the centre out with food.'

Minced Pork with Vermicelli

SERVES 2

- *300g minced pork*
- *½ cup (160g) GF oyster sauce*
- *2 spring onions, cut into 2 cm strips*
- *100g pkt GF bean vermicelli*

Combine mince, oyster sauce and spring onions. Refrigerate for approximately 1 hour. Soak vermicelli in warm water for 5–10 minutes until soft. Add marinated mince to a warm non-stick frying pan and stir fry until mince changes colour, break it up with a spatula. Lastly add vermicelli and stir fry quickly until noodles are heated. Serve immediately.

Onion Snags (Caramelised Sausages)

SERVES 2

- *4 thick GF sausages*
- *1 onion, sliced*
- *¼ cup (55g) brown sugar*
- *1 tomato, finely diced*

Cook sausages on a BBQ until done, and set aside to cool slightly. Place onions on a BBQ, cook till brown and sprinkle with sugar. Once onions have caramelised, score the sausages lengthways with a sharp knife and fill with onion and top with the diced tomato.

Paprika Chops

SERVES 2

- 2 large lean pork chops
- 2 tbs. (30ml) olive oil
- ½ tbs. paprika
- ½ tbs. white pepper

Heat oven to 200°C. Mix paprika and white pepper together. Season with a pinch of sea salt. Coat chops lightly with olive oil. Rub paprika and white pepper evenly over pork with fingers. Place both chops on a baking sheet and cook for 15–25 minutes or until juices run clear. Serve with vegies.

Pork & Coconut Satay Sticks

SERVES 4

In the words of Michelle Dodd: *"These are the best!"*

- 200ml coconut milk
- 2tbs. crunchy peanut butter
- 2tsp. GF curry powder
- 500g pork stir fry

Mix the first 3 ingredients together and season with sea salt and pepper until smooth and blended. Add the pork and marinate overnight. Soak 12 bamboo sticks in water before threading with the pork. Cook on a hot grill, turning constantly so as not to burn. Continue to glaze throughout.

Pork Fillets with Dried Fruit

SERVES 2 D.E.L.I.C.I.O.U.S!

- 1 cup (170g) dried mixed fruit
- 2 pork fillets
- ½ onion, chopped
- 2 rashers bacon

Preheat oven 180°C. Soak fruit in boiling water for 10 minutes or until plump and soft, then drain. Then cut a lengthways slit ¾ way through each fillet. Fry onion until brown and mix with fruit. Press into each fillet, wrap in bacon and tie with string. Seal each side for 1 minute in a non-stick frying pan, then bake in oven for 20 minutes.

Pork & Pumpkin Curry

SERVES 4

- ½ kg pork, cubed
- 2 tbs. GF red curry paste
- 410g can coconut cream
- ½ kg pumpkin, cubed

Over medium heat, brown pork in a large saucepan, add curry paste and stir, cooking for 5 minutes. Pour cream into pan, add ½ cup water and pumpkin, season to taste and bring to the boil. Reduce heat and simmer for 30 minutes or until the pork is cooked.

Optional: This is best made a few hours prior to serving as it thickens whilst cooling. Simply reheat when ready to serve.

Pork Roll

SERVES 4

- 500g GF pork sausages
- 1 free range egg
- 1 onion, grated
- 1 cup fresh GF breadcrumbs, browned

Prehat oven to 180°C. Cut skin from sausages. Mix pork, egg and onion together and season with sea salt and pepper. Form into a loaf and roll in GF breadcrumbs. Place in a baking dish and bake, turning after 20 minutes. After turning, cook for a further 20 minutes.

Optional: Serve with either apple or tomato sauce ... Surprisingly yummy!

Rich Tomato Pork

SERVES 4

A recipe from the lovely Tanya Ormsby.

- 4 pork chops
- 2 cloves garlic, crushed
- 420g can of seasoned diced tomatoes, e.g. basil and garlic or oregano and basil
- 125ml double cream

In a non-stick pan fry pork until golden on both sides, add garlic and tinned tomatoes, bring to boil then let simmer for 2½ hrs (you may need a little more tomato mixture, depending on size of fillets). Half an hour before serving, add cream and turn up the heat to thicken.

Optional: Serve with mashed potatoes and beans with pine nuts (see Vegetables).

Roast Pork

SERVES 8

From Lisa Darr. This continues to stand the test of time — a classic always does!

- *1 kg roast leg of pork*
- *3 tbs. (45ml) olive oil*

Preheat oven to 220°C. Place pork into a baking dish. Rub 1 tbs. oil onto rind of pork. Grind sea salt over rind and rub into flesh. Pour remaining oil into the dish and bake for 20 minutes. Reduce heat to 180°C and cook for 1 hour (or half hour per 500g).

Optional: Serve with roast vegetables, GF gravy and apple sauce.

Kim's husband, Glen, scores the skin and bathes it with fresh lemon juice and loads of ground sea salt to ensure a divine crackling!

Sausage Snacks

SERVES 4

A recipe from Errol McCosker.

- *4 large GF pork sausages*
- *4 tbs. GF sweet mustard pickle*
- *2 tbs. finely chopped chives or parsley (optional)*
- *2 cups mashed potato*

Grill or fry sausages, cool slightly then split open lengthways. Spread with pickle. Mix chives through mashed potato and spoon onto sausages, place under grill and cook until golden brown.

Optional: GF Sweet mustard pickle can be substituted for GF tomato sauce.

Spareribs

SERVES 6–8

- *2 kg pork spareribs*
- *200ml GF BBQ sauce*
- *1 orange, juiced*

Place ribs in a pot and cover with water. Simmer for 1 hour then drain. Place on a baking paper lined tray. Mix sauce and ⅔ cup juice and pour over the ribs. Bake in a 180°C oven for 30–40 minutes (until done to your liking) basting every 10 minutes.

Tangy Pork Chops

SERVES 4

- *4 pork chops*
- *½ cup (160g) honey*
- *¼ cup (60ml) GF Worcestershire sauce*
- *¼ cup (70g) tomato sauce*

Preheat oven to 170°C. Lightly brown pork chops under grill. Place in a shallow baking dish. Combine remaining ingredients and pour over chops. Cover and bake for 45 minutes.

Vegetarian Mains

Bite off more than you can chew, then chew it.
Plan more than you can do, then do it.

Anonymous

Asparagus Omelette

SERVES 4

Recipe by Janelle McCosker.

- *16 sticks of fresh asparagus*
- *2 tbs. (30g) butter*
- *8 free range eggs*
- *1 tsp. paprika*

Cut asparagus into 2 cm pieces. Melt butter in pan. Add asparagus and cook on medium heat until heated through. Beat eggs, season with sea salt and pepper and pour into non-stick frying pan. Add asparagus and cook over medium heat until eggs are set. Remove and place on platter, sprinkle with paprika.

Optional Fillings: *Classic: GF ham, tomato, mushroom, onion and cheese.*

Mid-Eastern: Crumbled goat's cheese and rocket

Asian: Crabmeat, coriander leaves and GF oyster sauce.

Mediterranean: Feta, olives and semi-dried tomatoes.

Aubergine & Ricotta Pasta

SERVES 4 Y.U.M.M.Y!

- *120g jar GF char-grilled, marinated aubergine*
- *500g jar GF tomato and basil passata*
- *375g GF penne pasta, cooked and drained*
- *250g fresh ricotta*

In a saucepan, add aubergine to passata and simmer for 10 minutes until warm. Divide pasta between 4 bowls and top with sauce and ricotta.

Aubergine & Sweet Potato Curry

SERVES 4

This is *really* delicious!

- *2 onions, peeled and sliced*
- *1 aubergine, chopped into 2 cm pieces*
- *1 medium to large size sweet potatoes, peeled and chopped into large chunks*
- *350g GF korma mildly spiced organic sauce*

Simmer onion in a little water for just a minute. Remove from pan and set aside. In a non-stick frying pan, fry aubergine until evenly browned. Add onions and sweet potato to pan with sweet potato and korma sauce. Fill half the empty jar with water and add to pan. Simmer for 20–30 minutes until the potato and aubergine are tender.

Optional: Serve with rice and pappadums.

Baked Ricotta & Thyme Pie

SERVES 6–8

This is super yummy served with a salad and delicious dressing!

- *1 kg fresh ricotta*
- *3 free range eggs, lightly beaten*
- *½ bunch of fresh thyme*
- *Olive oil spray*

Preheat oven 200°C. Spray a 22 cm round springform cake tin with oil. Place ricotta and eggs in a bowl and stir to combine. Using a spatula, pour mixture into tin and sprinkle generously with thyme and season. Bake for 35–40 minutes or until firm and golden. Allow to cool before removing from tin.

Optional: These can also be made in muffin trays. Reduce baking time to 15 minutes or until the pies are firm and golden.

Broccoli & Lemon Risotto

SERVES 2

- *1 bunch of broccoli*
- *1 cup (185g) arborio rice*
- *1 lemon*
- *50g parmesan cheese, grated*

Steam the broccoli florets until barely tender. Julienne the broccoli stems and sauté until just tender. Cook the rice in 1 ltr. of salty water, stirring regularly until all the liquid is absorbed. Grate the zest of the lemon into the rice, then add the juice of the lemon and ½ the parmesan. Stir to mix, add broccoli and mix gently. Season with sea salt and pepper and garnish with remaining parmesan.

Cheddar & Basil Tortillas

SERVES 1

- *1 tbs. (15g) butter*
- *2 soft GF tortillas*
- *50g cheddar cheese, grated*
- *¼ bunch of fresh basil leaves*

Heat butter in a non-stick frying pan over medium heat. Add one tortilla, layer with cheese then basil and season with sea salt and pepper, cook for 2 minutes or until underneath is golden brown. Top with remaining tortilla and flip. Cook for a further 2–3 minutes. Slide from pan onto a chopping board and cut into wedges. Serve immediately with a salad.

Optional: Substitute basil with semi-dried tomatoes, mushrooms, GF relish, whatever you like.

Coconut Rice

SERVES 4

- *1¼ cups (230g) basmati rice*
- *2 x 400ml cans coconut milk*
- *110g sultanas*

In a large pot over high heat, combine rice, coconut milk and 2 cups of water and bring to the boil. Reduce heat, add sultanas, cover and simmer on low heat for 25 minutes or until liquid is absorbed and rice is tender. Stir often.

Optional: Add a pinch of tumeric for colour.

Field Mushroom & Garlic Pizza

MAKES 2

Recipe from Rodger Fishwick.

- *2 GF wraps*
- *2 tsp. minced garlic*
- *100g field mushrooms, sliced*
- *50g mozzarella cheese, grated*

Preheat oven to 180°C. Place wraps on a baking paper lined tray. Spread minced garlic over the wrap and place the mushrooms on top. Sprinkle the mozzarella cheese over the top. Bake for 10 minutes.

Frittata

SERVES 4

A recipe by Katrina Price.

- *6 free range eggs*
- *1 small bunch of spinach, chopped*
- *100g parmesan cheese, grated*
- *½ cup (65g) GF breadcrumbs*

Preheat oven to 150°C. Beat the eggs with a whisk until light and fluffy, add spinach, cheese and GF breadcrumbs, season to taste. Line a baking tray with paper, pour in mixture and cook for 20 minutes.

Optional: Add cinnamon if desired (apparently it's good for the brain so we are using it to season EVERYTHING!!!)

Mixed Bean Korma

SERVES 4

- 420g can mixed beans, drained
- 125g fine green beans, cooked
- 500g jar GF creamy korma curry sauce
- 125g natural yoghurt

Place the mixed beans, green beans and korma sauce in a non-stick saucepan and simmer gently. Simmer for 10–15 minutes. Dollop with yoghurt and serve.

Nachos

SERVES 2

Recipe from Trudy Graham.

- 100g pkt GF corn chips
- ½ cup (85g) GF nachos supreme or salsa
- 70g cheddar cheese, grated
- ½ an avocado, mashed

Layer corn chips in a microwave safe dish. Top with salsa and cheese. Microwave until cheese melts, serve topped with mashed avocado.

Optional: Add some refried beans, diced tomato or sour cream. Rather than microwave, grill.

Polenta Cakes

SERVES 4

Inspired by Naomi Carter.

- *3 cups (750ml) GF vegetable stock*
- *1 cup (160g) polenta*
- *100g parmesan cheese, grated*
- *3 tbs. (45g) butter (reserve 1 for frying)*

In a saucepan, bring the stock to boil and stir in polenta. Continue stirring until mixture has thickened and is creamy. Add cheese and butter and mix well. Season with sea salt and pepper. Spoon polenta into a greased, round 20 cm cake tin and refrigerate until completely cold, then cut into 8 wedges. Heat in a non-stick frying pan and fry polenta each side until crisp and golden. For a little green, add some peas.

Potato Tortilla

SERVES 4

- *¼ cup (125ml) olive oil*
- *2 peeled and sliced potatoes*
- *8 free range eggs*

Heat olive oil in a non-stick frying pan over medium heat. Cook potatoes for 2–3 minutes. Whisk eggs together and season to taste. Pour over potatoes and cook for a further 10 minutes. Place under a hot grill for 2 minutes or long enough to brown. Allow to cool before cutting into wedges to serve.

Hint: To keep eggs fresh, store in fridge in their carton as soon as possible after purchase. This is because an egg will age more in a day at room temperature than it will in a week in the fridge.

Rice Pilaf

SERVES 4

A recipe from the lovely Fleur Whelligan.

- *1 onion, peeled and diced*
- *2 cloves garlic*
- *1 cup (185g) basmati rice*
- *2 cups (500ml) GF vegetable stock*

Preheat oven to 180°C. Sauté onion in a little water. Add garlic and rice and stir. Add stock and bring to the boil. Transfer mixture to a baking dish, cover and bake for 30 minutes. Remove from oven and fluff rice with fork.

Optional: Stir through a knob of butter and some chopped parsley if desired.

Spinach Pie

SERVES 2

A recipe from Karyn Turnbull-Markus.

- *1 small bunch of spinach, chopped*
- *250g cottage cheese*
- *1 clove garlic, crushed*
- *2 free range eggs, whisked*

Preheat oven to 180°C. Boil spinach for 5 minutes, drain and then in a small oven-proof dish, layer spinach, cottage cheese and garlic. After each layer, spoon over a little egg. Continue until all ingredients are used, ensuring final layer is cottage cheese then season with cracked pepper. Bake for 20 minutes or until pie is slightly brown on top.

Sweet Potato & Feta Frittata

SERVES 4

A fabulous dinner for anyone.

- *1 kg orange sweet potato, peeled and sliced 1 cm thick*
- *2 tbs. (30ml) olive oil*
- *200g feta, crumbled*
- *6 free range eggs*

Preheat oven to 200°C. Spread potato on a baking tray and sprinkle with half the oil. Bake for 20 minutes or until tender. Over medium heat, put remaining oil in a non-stick frying pan and add potato and feta. Whisk eggs and season with sea salt and pepper then pour over potato and feta. Reduce heat to low and cook for 5 minutes or until the base is set. Place frittata under medium preheated grill and grill for 7 minutes or until cooked through. Allow to cool slightly then cut into wedges.

Optional: This is delicious served with a fresh green salad.

Desserts

'It's not you, it's the dress!'

Beth from Bondi Markets, Sydney

Apple Crumble

SERVES 4–6

- 420g can pie apple
- ¾ cup (165g) brown sugar
- ½ cup (115g) soft butter
- 1 cup (175g) GF plain flour

Preheat oven to 200°C. Place apple filling into a baking dish. Sprinkle with 2 tbs. of brown sugar. Mix remaining ingredients in a bowl (reserving 2 tbs. butter) with a knife until crumbly. Sprinkle on top of apple filling and drizzle with reserved melted butter. Bake for 30 minutes, or until golden brown.

Optional: Add ½ tsp. mixed spice to the apple mix. Serve with custard or ice cream.

Baked Ricotta with Blueberry Sauce

SERVES 4

Kim's favourite! Dish this up to the applause of all!

- *2 free range egg whites*
- *⅓ cup (100g) honey*
- *250g ricotta cheese*
- *2 cups frozen blueberries, thawed*

Preheat oven to 180°C. Beat egg whites until stiff peaks form. Mix through 4 tbs. honey and ricotta cheese. Once combined, pour into a small, baking paper lined, oven-proof dish and bake for 40 minutes or until the pie rises and is golden. Meanwhile, place the berries in a small frying pan and heat gently until softened. Stir through 2 tbs. honey and allow to simmer for 20 minutes. Serve blueberry sauce over ricotta pie wedges.

Baked Rice Custard

SERVES 4

This is really easy and really tasty!

- *⅓ cup (60g) rice*
- *¾ can condensed milk*
- *3 free range eggs, lightly beaten*
- *¼ cup (40g) sultanas*

Preheat oven 180°C. Cook rice in a large pan of boiling water for 10 minutes, drain. Combine condensed milk, eggs, rice and sultanas with 1¾ cups water and mix thoroughly. Pour into a shallow ovenproof dish. Stand dish in baking pan with enough hot water to come halfway up sides of dish. Bake for 40 minutes or until set.

Optional: Before baking sprinkle with nutmeg.

Barbie Bananas

SERVES 4

A recipe from Tanya Ormsby.

- 4 bananas
- ½ cup (125ml) Baileys Irish Cream (or imitation)
- 4 scoops ice cream

Put the whole bananas on the BBQ — skins and all! Leave for 4–5 minutes, slit the top and add enough Baileys to prevent overflowing. Leave for a further 1–2 minutes, remove and serve with ice cream.

Blue Chockie Mousse

SERVES 4

This is berry, berry nice!

- 200g blueberries
- 200g dark chocolate
- 300ml double cream

Evenly place blueberries into the bottom of four small ramekins. Melt chocolate carefully in a bowl in the microwave, stir every 15 seconds. Remove and allow to cool. Beat cream until soft peaks form, then fold in the melted chocolate. Spoon the mixture over the blueberries and serve immediately.

Bread & Butter Pudding

SERVES 4

A recipe from Ralth Buttigieg. Sean, 7 and Rhys, 5, forgot about seconds, they wanted fourths!!!!!!

- 2 tbs. (30g) butter (a little extra for greasing)
- 5 slices thickly sliced GF raisin bread
- 2½ cups (625ml) milk
- 2 tbs. GF egg custard mix

Preheat oven 180°C. Butter the bread well and cut into fours. Layer into a greased, oven-proof dish. Mix the milk and custard powder until all the powder dissolves. Pour over bread. Allow at least ½ hour for the bread to soak up the liquid. Bake in oven until the top is golden brown. Allow to cool and enjoy!

Cheesecake Base

MAKES 1

- 155g pkt GF sweet biscuits
- ½ cup (85g) almond meal
- 4–5 tbs. (75g) butter, melted

Pop cookies into blender or processor and blend until fine. Pour into a bowl, add almond meal and melted butter and mix thoroughly. Pat into a greased or paper lined dish and chill.

Cheesecake Filling # 1

- *250g cream cheese*
- *200g tub vanilla yoghurt*
- *4 free range egg yolks*
- *2 cups mixed berries (if frozen, thawed)*

Preheat oven 180°C. Place cream cheese, yoghurt and egg yolks in a bowl. Mix until smooth then fold in the berries. Pour into a base and bake for 50 minutes.

Optional: Serve with Raspberry Sauce (see Sauces).

Cheesecake Filling # 2

- *250g cream cheese, softened*
- *400g condensed milk*
- *1 sachet gelatine*

In a medium bowl, beat cream cheese until smooth. Add condensed milk and beat until thick and creamy. Dissolve gelatine in 3 tbs. of boiling water, stirring vigorously until dissolved then add to the mixture. Mix thoroughly for 3 minutes to ensure gelatine spreads evenly throughout the mixture. Pour into a GF bickie base and chill for at least 2–3 hours, allowing time for the mixture to set, before serving.

Optional: This is pretty served topped with freshly sliced strawberries and kiwi fruit.

Chocolate Mousse Patty Cakes

MAKES 6

Recipe from Wendy King.

- *250g milk chocolate*
- *3 free range eggs*
- *¼ cup (45g) GF self raising flour*
- *300ml double cream, for serving*

Preheat oven to 180°C. Melt chocolate in a lightly heated saucepan stirring often to smooth. Mix eggs and flour with whisk and stir into chocolate. Place 6 patty cake papers into muffin tin and spoon in mixture. Bake for 20 minutes or until sides are set but centre is still liquid. Cool for 10 minutes. Carefully remove paper — centres will be a warm mousse consistency and serve dolloped with cream.

Optional: Sprinkle shaved chocolate on cream to make them look even MORE dazzling!

Chocolate Rum Cherries

MAKES 30

- *⅔ cup glace cherries*
- *¼ cup (60ml) dark rum*
- *90g dark chocolate, chopped*
- *½ cup (60g) pecans or walnuts, finely chopped*

Combine cherries and rum in bowl and stand overnight. Melt chocolate over hot water or in a microwave. Drain cherries, pat dry with absorbent paper, coat each cherry in chocolate. Sit for 1 minute, then sprinkle with nuts. Refrigerate until set.

Chocolate Panna Cotta

MAKES 4

So smooooooooooooooooooooth!

- *300ml cream*
- *200g good quality dark chocolate, chopped*
- *½ sachet gelatin*
- *1 tsp. vanilla essence*

Grease 4 x ½ cup ramekins and place on a baking tray. Place cream in a small saucepan. Stir over moderate heat for 1–2 minutes or until just boiling. Remove from heat, stir in chocolate until nice and smooth. Mix gelatine into 2 tbs. warm water and stir until dissolved. Stir gelatine and essence into cream mixture. Pour into prepared moulds. Cover with cling wrap and chill for at least 4 hours.

Hint: To serve, briefly dip base of mould into warm water, turn out onto serving plates.

Dark Chocolate Raspberry Fondue

SERVES 6–8

- *425g dark chocolate*
- *150ml double cream*
- *50g raspberries, pureed*
- *5 tbs. raspberry jam*

Break chocolate into pieces into a medium bowl. Add the cream (if you need more after it's all melted, then add more, you don't want it to be too thin) and add raspberry puree. Microwave on medium high stirring every 30 seconds until mixture is nice and smooth. Stir in jam and more cream if desired. Place in fondue pot and serve with dippers of your choice.

Frozen Fruit Yoghurt Soft Serve

SERVES 4–6

A recipe from Cyndi O'Meara.

- *2 cups fresh fruit (bananas, strawberries, mango, blueberries, etc.), all roughly chopped*
- *½ cup (160g) honey*
- *500g natural yoghurt*

Process fruit in a blender until smooth. Add honey and yoghurt and mix thoroughly. Pour into a covered container and freeze. Remove from freezer 20–30 minutes before serving.

Orange Ricotta Puddings

MAKES 4

These are fabulous!

- *300g fresh ricotta cheese*
- *⅓ cup (65g) caster sugar*
- *½ cup (125ml) GF custard*
- *1 orange, zest and juice*

Place ricotta and sugar in a bowl and beat until smooth. Add custard, ½ cup (125ml) juice and 2 tbs. of orange zest, beat until well combined. Spoon into serving bowls or glasses and top with fresh orange segments. Refrigerate for 30 minutes before serving.

Pavlova

SERVES 6–8

- *4 free range egg whites*
- *1 cup (200g) caster sugar*
- *2 tsp. maize cornflour*
- *1 tsp. vanilla essence*

Preheat the oven to 180°C. Line a baking tray with baking paper. Beat the egg whites until soft peaks form and gradually beat in the sugar. Beat until the mixture is thick and the sugar is dissolved. Carefully fold in the cornflour and vanilla essence. Spoon onto the baking paper on the tray. Reduce the oven heat to 150°C and place in oven to bake for 1 hour.

Hint: For best result, eggs should be at room temperature.

Peanut Butter Ice Cream Pie

SERVES 6–8

- *200g pkt GF chocolate chip cookies, finely crumbled*
- *75g butter, melted*
- *1 ltr. creamy vanilla ice cream, softened*
- *1¼ cups (325g) crunchy peanut butter*

In a bowl, mix biscuit crumbs and melted butter. Press into a paper lined pie dish and chill. Beat ice cream and peanut butter in a large bowl with an electric beater until nice and smooth. Pour into chilled biscuit base and place in freezer for at least 3 hours prior to serving.

Optional: Serve drizzled with Hot Fudge Sauce (see Sauces).

Pears in Coffee Syrup

SERVES 4

These are easy and economical especially when in season.

- ½ cup (110g) sugar
- 2 tsp. instant coffee
- 4 pears, peeled

In a saucepan combine the sugar and coffee with 2 cups of water and stir over a low heat until the sugar is dissolved. Add the pears and simmer until they are soft. To serve, place pears in individual bowls and pour the syrup around them.

Plum Pudding

SERVES 6

A recipe from Daphne Beutel ... This is a KNOCKOUT!

- 2½ cups (440g) GF self raising flour
- 1 cup (220g) sugar
- 1 kg pkt dried mixed fruit
- 1 tbs. bicarbonate of soda

Mix first 3 ingredients together in a large bowl. Add 2 cups of hot water and bi-carbonate of soda, mix with a knife, cover and leave overnight. Mix well the next morning. Place in a GF floured cloth and boil for 3 hours.

Roasted Honey Pears with Honey Cream

SERVES 4

- 3 firm, ripe pears
- ½ cup (160g) honey
- 2 tbs. brown sugar
- 300ml double cream, whipped

Preheat oven to 180°C. Cut pears into quarters and remove cores. Place in an ovenproof dish, drizzle with ¼ cup honey and sprinkle with brown sugar. Pour ½ cup water around pears. Bake uncovered for 30 minutes or until just soft. Place 3 pear quarters on four serving plates. Drizzle pan juices over pears. Mix whipped cream and ¼ cup honey together until combined. Serve over pears.

Optional: Add ¼ tsp. cinnamon to cream and honey for a lovely flavour.

Rum & Raisin Ice cream

SERVES 4

- 1 cup (170g) raisins
- ½ cup (125ml) dark rum
- 2 ltr. GF creamy vanilla ice cream

Pop raisins and rum into a saucepan over medium heat and bring to a simmer. Remove from heat and cool completely. Process raisin mixture until roughly chopped. Fold through softened ice cream. Cover with cling wrap, seal with the lid and freeze overnight before serving.

Stuffed Apples

MAKES 4 ...YUMMMMMMMY!!!

- 4 large green apples
- 100g leftover GF fruitcake or GF Christmas pudding

Preheat oven to 180°C. Core apples and wrap in aluminium foil and bake for 20 minutes. Remove aluminium foil and stuff with fruitcake, bake for a further 10 minutes. Serve warm with GF custard.

Optional: Can sprinkle with cinnamon or substitute fruit cake for sultanas as Kim's Nana, Mary Moore, has been doing for decades!

Soy Custard

SERVES 4

- 5 free range egg yolks
- ⅓ cup (80g) pure maple syrup
- 2 cups (500ml) GF soy milk

Whisk egg yolks with maple syrup in a bowl. Warm the soy milk in a saucepan. Add the egg and maple mixture to the milk. Return the saucepan to a medium heat and stir constantly until the mixture thickens.

Sticky Mango Rice

SERVES 6

This is delectable!

- 1 cup (185g) short grain rice
- ½ cup (110g) sugar
- 375ml can coconut cream
- 3 mangoes, peeled and sliced

Place rice with 1¾ cups water into a saucepan and bring to the boil. Reduce heat, cover and cook for approximately 10 minutes. Add sugar and 1 cup of coconut cream stirring until combined and rice is nice and soft. Dollop mixture into serving bowls and serve with mango drizzled with remaining coconut cream.

Optional: Substitute mangoes for lychees.

Srawberry & Banana Skewers with Caramel Dip

MAKES 12

One loved by all!

- 400g can Carnation caramel
- ⅓ cup (80ml) cream
- 500g strawberries, washed and hulled
- 2 bananas, peeled and sliced

Pour caramel and cream into a saucepan, bring to the boil and reduce heat, simmering for 2–3 minutes. Pour mixture into a jug, allow to cool. Thread strawberries and banana alternatively onto skewers and drizzle with sauce when ready to serve.

Tropical Fruit Salad

SERVES 4

Simply Scrumptious!

- *1 ripe mango, diced*
- *8 lychees, peeled and quartered*
- *1 banana, peeled and sliced*
- *The fruit of 3 passionfruits*

Combine all and mix. Delicious served with ice cream or as an accompaniment to a sweet.

All I Really Need to Know I Learned in Kindergarten

(a guide for Global Leadership)

An excerpt from the book,
All I Really Need To Know I Learned in Kindergarten.

By Robert Fulghum
www.robertfulghum.com

All I really need to know about how to live, and what to do, and how to be, I learned in kindergarten. Wisdom was not at the top of the graduate school mountain, but there in the sand pile at school.

These are the things I learned:

- Share everything

- Play fair

- Don't hit people

- Put things back where you found them

- Clean up your own mess

- Don't take things that are not yours

- Say you're sorry when you hurt somebody

- Wash your hands before you eat

- Flush

- Warm cookies and cold milk are good for you

- Live a balanced life — learn some and think some and draw and paint and sing and dance and play and work every day some

- Take a nap every afternoon

- When you go out in the world, watch out for traffic, hold hands and stick together

- Be aware of wonder. Remember the little seed in the Styrofoam cup: the roots go down and the plant goes up and nobody really knows how or why, but we are all like that

- Goldfish and hamsters and white mice and even the little seed in the Styrofoam cup — they all die. So do we.

- And then remember the Dick-and-Jane books and the first word you learned — the biggest word of all — **LOOK!**

Take any one of those items and extrapolate it into sophisticated adult terms and apply it to your family life or your work or government or your world and it holds true and clear and firm.

Think what a better world it would be if we all — **the whole world** — had cookies and milk at about 3 o'clock in the afternoon and then lay down with our blankies for a nap. Or if all governments had as a basic policy to always put things back where they found them and to clean up their own mess.

And it is still true, no matter how old you are, when you go out in the world, it is best to hold hands and stick together!

For The Children

The best thing a father can do for his children is to love their mother!

Unknown

Savoury

BBQ Chicken Pizza

MAKES 2

- *2 GF wraps*
- *4 tbs. GF BBQ sauce*
- *200g roasted chicken, shredded*
- *½ cup (50g) mozzarella cheese, grated*

Preheat oven to 180°C. Divide sauce and spread evenly over each wrap. Top with chicken and sprinkle with cheese. Bake for 10 minutes or until cheese is melted and lightly browned.

* Optional Fillings: Add ham and finely chopped bacon for 'Meatlovers'

Add thinly sliced mushrooms and substitute BBQ sauce for pizza sauce for 'Funghi'

Add a mezze of antipasto for 'Vegetarian'

Put it on a pizza and they will eat it!!

Chicken Carnival Cones

MAKES 8

A recipe by Isobele *'Pruuuu'* Whiting that is enjoyed by EVERYONE!

- *8 GF tortillas*
- *2 cups leftover chicken meat, shredded*
- *1 cup (175g) salsa*
- *100g cheddar cheese, grated*

Preheat oven to 180°C. Fold tortilla in half (if small, fold only the bottom third up) and roll into a cone. Fill bottom of cone with chicken, dollop 2 generous tsp. of salsa before covering with a layer of cheese. Place on a paper lined baking tray and repeat the process until all ingredients are used. Bake for 15 minutes.

Chicken, Mango & Chickpea Burgers

MAKES 12

- *400g chickpeas, drained*
- *500g lean chicken mince*
- *4–5 tbs. GF mango chutney*
- *2 spring onions, finely chopped*

Process chickpeas, combine with remaining ingredients and season. Shape into patties and cook in a non-stick frying pan over a moderate heat for 3 minutes. Flip and cook for another 3 minutes or until cooked through. Serve on a fresh roll with a slice of tomato and lettuce.

Chicken Nuggets # 1

SERVES 4

- *100g corn polenta*
- *1 tsp. dried sage*
- *500g chicken, cut into bite size pieces*
- *½ cup (125ml) olive oil*

Mix polenta and sage in a plastic bag, then pop in chicken pieces. Toss them around to gain an even coating. Add ½ cup of oil to a non-stick frying pan and heat until really hot. Place the coated chicken in, fry for about 1 minute per side then remove from pan. Use extra oil if needed.

Chicken Nuggets # 2

SERVES 4

- *500g chicken cut into bite size pieces*
- *½ cup (130g) GF mayonnaise*
- *1 cup instant GF potato flakes*

Preheat oven to 200°C. Line baking tray with baking paper. Place mayo and potato flakes onto 2 separate plates. Roll chicken first into mayo and then into potato flakes. Pop the coated pieces onto a paper lined baking tray and bake for 20 minutes or until done. Flip once to brown evenly.

Chicken Patties

MAKES 10

- 3–4 slices GF white bread, crusts off
- 500g chicken mince
- 150g mozzarella cheese, grated
- 1 free range egg yolk

Pour 1 cup (250ml) of water onto a tray and place bread into it, just so that it is wet through. Squeeze liquid out of bread and pop it into a bowl with the rest of the ingredients and mix to combine. Roll into patties and pan fry in a non-stick frying pan until golden on both sides.

Creamy Meatballs

SERVES 4–6

- 750g extra lean mince
- 250g sour cream
- 1 tsp. garlic salt
- 2 tbs. (30ml) olive oil

Combine first 3 ingredients in a bowl. Roll into patties. Allow oil to heat in a non-stick frying pan and then fry patties over a medium heat.

Optional: Roll in GF breadcrumbs before frying.

Easy Pork Bites

MAKES 36

A recipe from the brilliant Michelle Dodd.

- *6 GF flavoured sausages eg. Italian, herb and garlic, honey and rosemary, rosemary and lamb ... Whatever takes your fancy!*

Preheat oven to 180°C. Squeeze the contents of sausages into a bowl. Roll into bite-sized balls and bake for 15 minutes. Serve warm with your favourite sauce.

Fish Pie

SERVES 4

A Turnbull household staple ... Yummy!

- *350g organic tomato and GF basil pasta sauce*
- *4 white fish fillets, cut into chunks*
- *4 potatoes*
- *100g cheddar cheese, grated*

Over medium heat pour sauce into a non-stick frying pan. Allow to warm, then add fish, cook for 8 minutes or until fish is done. Remove from heat and allow to sit before pouring into a baking dish. Meanwhile peel, cut, boil and mash potatoes. Spread over fish mixture and sprinkle generously with cheese. Grill until cheese has melted and turned a lovely golden colour.

Optional: This is delicious served with a variety of fresh steamed vegies.

Frankfurt Pasta Bake

SERVES 4–6

- 6 GF frankfurters, quartered
- 2 cups cooked GF pasta spirals
- 420g jar of GF pasta bake sauce
- 1 cup grated cheese

Preheat oven to 180°C. Mix frankfurters, pasta and sauce together. Spoon the mixture into a baking dish and sprinkle with cheese. Bake for 20 minutes.

Healthy Hotdogs

SERVES 4

- 4 GF wraps
- 4 GF sausages
- 100g cheddar cheese, grated
- 1 carrot, peeled and grated

Grill or BBQ the sausages. Lay wraps out and sprinkle equal portions of cheese onto each. Add chosen vegetable and roll up.

Optional: Serve with tomato or GF BBQ sauce.

Honey Drummies

SERVES 2

Recipe from mighty mummy Michelle Ashdown.

- *4 chicken drumsticks*
- *2 tbs. honey*
- *2 tbs. (30ml) pear juice*
- *1 tsp. olive oil*

Preheat oven to 180°C. Place chicken drumsticks into an airtight container and mix all other ingredients and ½ tsp. sea salt. Pour over chicken. Marinate for 4 hours before placing onto a baking paper lined tray and cooking for 40 minutes in oven. Spoon over juices twice during cooking process and serve with vegies or rice.

Hummus Sausages

SERVES 2

Soooooo quick and easy — recipe by the very suave Tony Van Dijk.

- *4 GF herbed or Italian sausages*
- *4 tsp. hummus*
- *1 lemon, quartered*

Grill or sauté the sausage and serve with a dollop of hummus and a lemon wedge.

Lasagne

SERVES 4–6. RECIPE BY DAN PRIMMER.

"Without white sauce?" You ask. "Try it! " We reply!

- *500g mince*
- *500g jar GF pasta sauce*
- *6 GF lasagne sheets*
- *100g mozzarella cheese, grated*

Preheat oven to 180°C. In a non-stick pan cook mince over low heat. When browned add pasta sauce, season and stir and allow to simmer. In a medium sized baking dish spoon half the mince into the dish, place 3 *dampened* lasagne sheets on top and sprinkle with cheese. Repeat the process until all ingredients are used. Press gently to ensure pasta sheets are in contact with liquid. Cover with aluminium foil and place in oven for 45–50 minutes or until pasta has softened.

Tip: We often buy mince in 2 kg quantities to get the 'buy in bulk' discount. We ask our butchers to pack it in 500g lots as that is what suits our sized families.

Mini Cheese Quiches

SERVES 4

- *4 GF tortillas*
- *2 large free range eggs, lightly beaten*
- *½ cup grated cheddar cheese*
- *1 tbs. mixed herbs*

Preheat oven to 210°C. Using a large scone cutter, cut out 3 rounds from each tortilla. Line the base of a non-stick muffin tin with tortilla rounds (dampen slightly to help mould if needed). Fill each cup with cheese and herbs and a sprinkle of pepper. Top each with egg mixture and bake for 15 minutes or until set.

Mouse Traps

SERVES 1

Recipe by Wendy King.

- 2 slices day old GF bread
- 1 slice GF shortcut bacon, cut in half
- 2 slices tasty cheese

Remove the sides off the GF bread. Lay a slice of cheese on each piece of GF bread and top with a slice of bacon on each. Place under grill and cook until bacon is crispy. Cut length ways into 3 fingers and serve.

Peanut Butter Toasties

SERVES 2

- 2 slices GF bread
- 2 tbs. peanut butter
- 2 tbs. sultanas
- 30g cheddar cheese, grated

Grill one side of the GF bread slices until golden. Turn and spread with peanut butter then sprinkle with sultanas and top with grated cheese. Grill until cheese is melted, cut in half to serve.

Potato Bake

SERVES 2–4

- *2 large potatoes*
- *½ cup (125ml) cream*
- *½ cup (125ml) milk*
- *1 tbs. nutmeg*

Preheat oven to 180°C. Finely slice potatoes and layer in a greased pie dish. Mix cream and milk together and pour over potatoes. Sprinkle with nutmeg and bake for ½ hr or until golden brown.

Roma Chicken

SERVES 4

A recipe from Katrina Price — your children will *loooooove* this!

- *½ a cooked chicken, remove skin*
- *500g of your favourite GF tomato based pasta sauce*
- *1 red pepper, de-seeded and sliced*
- *2 tbs. sour cream*

Shred chicken and mix with sauce and pepper in a non-stick frying pan. Season to taste and simmer until pepper is cooked. Stir in sour cream at the end and serve over rice.

Savoury Muffins

MAKES 26 MINI-MUFFINS OR 12 LARGE

Recipe by Dymphna Boholt.

- *2 cups (350g) of GF self raising flour*
- *2 free range eggs*
- *150g cheddar cheese, grated*
- *1 cup (250ml) milk*

Preheat oven to 200°C. Mix all ingredients together and dollup into mini-muffin trays. Bake for 17 minutes for mini-muffins or 26 minutes for the larger ones.

Shepherd's Pie with a Twist

SERVES 6

Hamilton, 4, often asks for 'Pie' meaning this for dinner!

- *500g minced steak*
- *680g can GF spaghetti in tomato sauce*
- *3 large potatoes, peeled, boiled and mashed*
- *75g cheddar cheese, grated*

Preheat oven to 180°C. Brown mince in a non-stick frying pan until cooked (drain excess liquid if any). Add spaghetti, season and mix well. Simmer for 10 minutes. Pour into a casserole dish, top with potato and grated cheese. Bake for 15 minutes or until cheese is golden brown. Serve with vegies of choice.

Tacos

MAKES 2

- *2 GF taco shells*
- *1 cup lean beef mince*
- *⅓ cup (80g) GF pasta sauce*
- *1 cup shredded lettuce*

Cook mince in a non-stick frying pan till pink has disappeared and add pasta sauce. Simmer on low heat for 5 minutes. Alternate a thin layer of mince with a thin layer of lettuce till each taco is full.

Optional: You can also add sliced mushrooms, peas and shredded carrot to the mince meat mix too.

Yummy Bean Grill

MAKES 2

- *130g can GF baked beans*
- *1–2 tbs. finely chopped parsley*
- *2 slices GF bread, lightly toasted*
- *2 thin slices mozzarella cheese*

Combine beans and parsley and spread over toast. Top with mozzarella and place under preheated grill until cheese melts.

Sweet

Life is a series of moments. To live each one is to succeed.

Corita Kent

Apricot Dream Balls

MAKES 24

Paul Bermingham's favourites!

- *120g dried mixed fruit*
- *40g dried apricots*
- *1 tbs. coconut milk*
- *½ cup (60g) dessicated coconut*

Place fruit medley, apricots and coconut milk into a food processor or your hand-held mixer, and whiz until mixture comes together. Shape into balls and roll in coconut. Chill until firm.

Caramel Biscuits

MAKES 24

- *200g softened butter*
- *½ cup (110g) brown sugar*
- *2 tbs. golden syrup*
- *1 cup (175g) GF self raising flour*

Preheat oven to 180°C. Cream butter and sugar. Add syrup and beat until fluffy. Mix in GF flour until texture is such that you are able to roll into balls. Place on a baking paper lined tray and allow for spreading, press each gently with a fork and bake for 15 minutes.

Chocolate Balls

A recipe by Grandma McCosker and loved by Matthew, Brady & Harry!

- *200g pkt GF sweet biscuits*
- *3 tbs. cocoa or GF drinking chocolate*
- *¾ cup condensed milk*
- *½ cup (60g) dessicated coconut*

Pop cookies into a blender and blend until finely crushed. Pour into a bowl and mix biscuit, cocoa and condensed milk together to make a thick, sticky consistency. Using a generous tsp. of mixture, roll into balls and cover in coconut. Chill before serving. These can also be frozen.

Optional: Sustagen can be used instead of cocoa or drinking chocolate and is a great dose of fibre for growing bodies!

Tip: Wet hands make rolling these much easier. If too sticky, add more biscuits.

Chocolate Dipped Fruit

SERVES 4

- *200g chocolate melts*
- *2 bananas, thickly sliced*
- *200g strawberries, washed and hulled*
- *¾ cup dried apricots*

Line baking tray with baking paper. Place melts in microwave-safe bowl and cook on high, stirring every 15 seconds, until melted. Using your hand, dip fruit, one piece at a time, into chocolate to coat about half of each piece. Place on paper-lined baking tray, refrigerate until set.

Chocolate Marshmallow Truffles

MAKES 24

- 250g pkt GF marshmallows
- 400g choc chips, melted
- 50g flaked almonds, finely chopped

Dip marshmallows one at a time in melted chocolate, turning to coat evenly. Gently shake off excess chocolate and place in single layers on a paper lined baking tray. Sprinkle all with almonds. Set in the refrigerator before enjoying!

Chocolate Toffee

MAKES 24

- 2½ cups (550g) sugar
- 125g butter
- ¼ tsp. cream of tartar
- 125g dark chocolate, finely chopped

Combine sugar, butter and cream of tartar in saucepan. Add ⅔ cup water, stir constantly over heat until sugar dissolves. Boil for 2–3 minutes. Remove from heat immediately and quickly stir in chocolate. Pour mixture into 24 paper lined mini-muffin trays and allow to set in the fridge.

Egg Custard

MAKES 2 CUPS

Grandma McCosker used to make this with prune snow (see p. 213) — delicious!

- *2 cups (500ml) milk*
- *5 tbs. caster sugar*
- *2 free range egg yolks*
- *2 tbs. maize cornflour*

Bring the milk and 2 tbs. sugar to boil in a saucepan over a medium heat. Whisk the yolks and remaining sugar together, then gradually fold in the cornflour to form a pale yellow paste. Carefully pour half of the boiled milk into the yolk mixture, whisking to incorporate. Return the remaining milk to the heat and bring to the boil, quickly whisk in the yolk mixture. Continue mixing until it returns to the boil. Transfer to a clean, dry bowl and cover the surface with cling wrap. Chill until required.

Hint: To use the custard once it has been chilled, beat until smooth. An electric beater gives a much smoother result than beating by hand.

Fruit Dip

MAKES 1 CUP

- *250g Greek yoghurt*
- *½ tsp. ground cinnamon*
- *3 tbs. fruit jam*

Place all ingredients into a bowl and mix well. Chill for at least 2 hours prior to serving to allow flavours time to develop. Serve with a platter of fresh fruit for dipping.

Fruit Medley

SERVES 8

- 4 nectarines, chopped
- 2 bananas, sliced
- 100g blueberries
- 1 tbs. (15ml) orange juice

Combine all ingredients in a bowl and gently toss. Cool in fridge before serving.

Fruit Kebabs

SERVES 4–6

Recipe from Jen Whittington.

- 1 pkt skewers
- Choice of 2 fruits (berries, melon, citrus; whatever you have in the fridge or in the fruit basket)
- Choice of 1 tub of fruit yoghurt or 1 tbs. of organic honey

Dice fruit into bite-size pieces (skin and clean, where required). Thread the chosen fruits alternatively onto a skewer, leaving enough room at the base so the skewer can be held. Drizzle with yoghurt or honey.

Honey & Cornflake Cookies

MAKES 24

This is Jaxson's number 1 favourite cookie!

- *150g butter*
- *½ cup (160g) honey*
- *2 cups (370g) GF self raising flour*
- *2½ cups (300g) GF cornflakes*

Preheat oven to 180°C. In a small saucepan combine butter and honey and mix over a low heat. Combine flour and cornflakes in a bowl, pour in butter mixture and stir to combine. Using a tablespoon, roll mixture into balls and lay onto 2 paper-lined baking trays. With a fork, flatten slightly. Bake for 10 minutes or until golden. Cool on trays.

Tip: For best storage place a layer of baking paper between layers and keep in an airtight container.

Jam Drops

MAKES 60

Recipe by Joy Duke.

- *230g butter, softened*
- *½ cup (100g) caster sugar*
- *2 cups (350g) GF plain flour*
- *Jam of choice*

Preheat oven to 195°C. Cream butter and sugar until light and fluffy. Fold in GF flour and spoon into heaped dollops onto a baking paper-lined tray. Use the end of a wooden spoon to push a hole through to the base of the biscuit dough. Fill hole with jam of choice and bake for 15 minutes or until slightly golden. Remove from oven and allow to cool before serving.

Kisses

MAKES 24

- *115g butter, softened (reserve a tsp.)*
- *1 cup (175g) GF self raising flour*
- *1 tbs. GF icing sugar*
- *1 tbs. arrowroot*

Preheat oven to 150°C. Cream butter and sugar first before adding arrowroot and flour. Line a baking tray with baking paper, roll a teaspoon full into a ball, place on tray and press with a fork. Place in oven and bake for 10 minutes or until golden brown.

Optional: Join two together with some jam or icing when cold.

Mallow Pears

MAKES 4

A recipe by Justine Ormsby.

- *2 pears, halved and deseeded*
- *8 GF marshmallows (or lots of GF mini marshmallows)*
- *¼ tsp. nutmeg*

Place pear halves on a microwave safe dish, cover and microwave for 1 minute. Remove and top each pear with 2 marshmallows and a sprinkle of nutmeg. Grill under moderate heat until marshmallows are golden brown. Serve warm.

Melon Ice Blocks

MAKES 8

- 4 cups chopped, seedless watermelon
- 2 cups chopped fresh pineapple

Combine all ingredients and blend, in batches, until smooth. Pour into iceblock moulds and freeze.

Optional: Watermelon can be substituted with 2 cups of honeydew melon.

Muesli Slice

MAKES 12

- ½ cup (115g) butter
- 3 cups (330g) GF muesli
- ½ cup (160g) golden syrup

Line a lamington tray with non-stick baking paper. Melt butter in a medium saucepan, add muesli and syrup, stirring over a medium heat for about 5 minutes or until mixture thickens and is dark golden brown. Spread over base of prepared pan. Cover and refrigerate to set. Slice into desired portions.

Orange Delight

MAKES 2 AND IS IDEAL FOR AN AFTER SCHOOL SNACK.

- 2 oranges

Insert a paddle pop stick into a peeled orange, wrap with plastic wrap and freeze for an hour or two.

Patty Cakes (Fairy Cakes)

MAKES 24

Your children will *devour* these.

- *125g butter, softened*
- *¾ cup (150g) caster sugar*
- *3 free range eggs*
- *2 cups (350g) GF self raising flour*

Preheat oven to 160°C. Combine ingredients with ¼ cup (60ml) water in a bowl. Beat with an electric beater on low until just combined. Then beat on medium until mixture is nice and smooth. Dollop across 2 patty paper-lined patty tins and bake for 20 minutes.

Optional: Yummy iced with mock cream.

Peppermint Chocolate Slice

MAKES AROUND 21 PIECES

This is BRILLIANT and so very easy the kids can do it!

- *200g dark chocolate melts*
- *3 drops peppermint essence*
- *100g white chocolate melts*
- *4 drops green food colouring*

Line 20 cm square cake tin with baking paper or aluminium foil. Melt dark chocolate melts in a lightly heated saucepan, stirring throughout melting process. Add peppermint essence and stir. Spread half the mixture evenly over bottom of tin. Set in fridge for 5 minutes. Melt white chocolate melts the same way then stir in green food colouring. Spread this over layer of dark chocolate and then refrigerate until set. Spread remaining dark chocolate over white/green chocolate and set in fridge. Cut into pieces and store in fridge.

Prune Snow

SERVES 4

- 1 cup prunes
- 2 tbs. caster sugar
- 2 free range egg whites

Place prunes into a saucepan and cover with water. Cook for approximately 10 minutes, or until soft. Remove from heat and allow to cool. Meanwhile, beat egg whites until fluffy, add sugar gradually and continue to beat until stiff. Remove seeds from prunes, and mash. Fold eggwhites into prunes and serve with custard.

Note: you can use your egg yolks to make a delicious egg custard (see Desserts).

Rice Pudding

SERVES 4

A recipe from the beautiful Mary Moore, great-grandmother to 16.

- 1 ltr. milk
- ½ cup (90g) rice
- 2 tbs. sugar
- ½ tsp. vanilla essence

Preheat oven to 150°C. Add all ingredients to a baking dish, place in the middle of oven and bake for 1½ hours.

Rocky Road Ice cream

A fantastic version from the wonderful Wendy Beattie.

- *200g pkt GF chocolate biscuits, chopped*
- *200g pkt GF marshmallows*
- *1 cup GF red raspberry lollies*
- *2 ltr. GF chocolate ice cream, softened*

Fold the first 3 ingredients through the ice cream. Smooth the top before covering with cling wrap. Freeze overnight.

Optional: Serve sprinkled with more marshmallows and shaved chocolate.

Vanilla Ice Cream

A terrific little recipe by the gorgeous Carly Nelson, Noosaville.

- *600ml double cream, whipped lightly*
- *3 cups (750ml) full cream milk*
- *2 tbs. vanilla*
- *1½ cups (300g) sugar*

Mix all ingredients together until thoroughly combined. Place in freezer for at least 4 hours prior to serving. Easy and cheap!

Optional: Mix in some flaked chocolate or fresh fruit for variety — everyone will love it!

Gluten Free Lunchboxes

*To bring up a child in the way he should go
travel that way yourself once in a while.*

Josh Billings

We are mothers with little boys who eat and eat and eat! When it comes to lunchboxes, sometimes it's hard enough, trying to find the balance between good nutrition and including foods the kids will eat, without having to look for gluten free options too!!!

There are lots of ways to pack a healthy gluten free school lunch. Start by getting your children involved in the weekly menu planning process, this generally increases the odds that they will actually eat what you pack for them!

According to The Australian Coeliac December 2008 magazine, a lunch box should always include:

✓ *At least 2 pieces of fruit or vegetables (fresh, dried or tinned)*

✓ *At least 1 serve of dairy food such as yoghurt, milk or cheese*

✓ *At least 3–4 serves carbohydrate rich foods such as bread, crispbread, grain and fruit based bars, pasta, etc.*

✓ *At least 1 serve of protein*

The recommended serves from each food group varies with age. If you are unsure what your child requires, you may want to seek advice from a dietitian.

Here are 25 of our favourite suggestions of what to include in a lunchbox gathered from far and wide, from people just like you and us are:

1. *Start by utilizing leftovers*

2. *Fruit – make it easier to eat. Remove orange peel or cut a kiwi fruit in half and include a spoon in the lunchbox*

---

3. Fruit Kebabs – pineapple, rockmelon, honeydew, apple, grapes, oranges and strawberries are all great chopped and threaded onto a skewer

4. Fruit pieces with yoghurt to dip into, add a dash of cinnamon to the yoghurt

5. Dried fruit, in season dry your own mango … The children will love it!

6. Banana chips lightly dipped in chocolate

7. Vegetables – raw vegetables cut into slices, or florets are fabulous as dipping sticks for your child's favourite dip. Our children love the gherkin dip and the Avo & Corn Dip

8. Celery sticks, stuffed with peanut butter and sprinkled with sultanas. Or if peanut butter is a no-go, try cottage cheese

9. Cheese cubes served with your favourite GF crackers, rice crackers or GF pretzels

10. Pancake or pikelet, add the zest of an orange or lemon for citrus pancakes

11. Plain popcorn (add a small amount of dried fruit for variety)

12. Cinnamon Popcorn … This is delish! In a small saucepan, melt 2 tbs. butter, then add 1 tbs. brown sugar and ½ tsp. cinnamon drizzle over bowl of plain popcorn and toss to mix

13. Creamed rice with fruit

14. Microwaved pappadums

15. Homemade tortilla chips cut into triangles, sprinkle with a little parmesan cheese and bake at 180°C for 15–20 minutes or until crisp

16. GF sausages cut into bite size pieces

17. Chicken drumsticks

18. Fish cakes, made with tins of tuna or salmon, egg, potato and peas are yummy!

19. Corn tortillas for roll-up sandwiches; ham, cheese and shredded lettuce, hummus, cheese and thinly sliced tomato

20. Corn tortillas for pizza bases:

Margarita: Pizza sauce, fresh basil and mozzarella

Hawaiian: Pizza sauce, GF ham, pineapple and mozzarella

Pepperoni: Pizza sauce, GF pepperoni and mozzarella

Italian: Pizza sauce, olives, GF salami and mozzarella

Mexican: Salsa, avocado, sour cream and mozzarella

21. GF Corn chips with guacamole, and that can be as simple as a mashed avocado with a dollop of salsa and a dollop of sour cream

22. Lettuce wraps; fill an iceberg lettuce leaf with GF shredded ham and grated cheese and gently roll it, wrap it with a chive or seal it with a toothpick to hold it together

23. Parmesan crisps (see Cocktail Food) … Your children will looooove these served with their favourite dips

24. Almond Muffins (see Morning & Afternoon Teas) add a variety of fruit to the mix to vary the flavour

25. Chocolate Balls – our little boys loooooooooooooooooooove it when these turn up by surprise in their lunchboxes. Take a 155g pkt GF cookies, blend, add condensed milk and GF cocoa powder roll into balls and then into dessicated coconut (see Sweet). These freeze well too so make a STACK!!!

Gluten free need not be taste free!

The Australian Coeliac Society

For The Baby & Toddlers

A baby will make love stronger
Days shorter, nights longer
Bank roll smaller
Home happier, clothes shabbier
The past forgotten
And the future worth living for.

Anonymous

Bananavo

Recipe by Kim Morrison. *This is tops!*

- ¼ avocado
- ¼ banana

Mash and combine well together and serve.

Brazilian Fried Bananas

- 1 banana, thickly sliced
- 1 tbs. (15g) butter
- 1 tbs. cinnamon sugar

Melt butter in a small frying pan over medium heat. Add banana slices and fry until just starting to toast, turn and fry until both sides are golden brown. Sprinkle with cinnamon sugar, allow to caramelise. Remove from pan and serve warm.

Optional: These are delish served drizzled with GF custard.

Broccoli & Cheddar Nuggets

- ½ head of broccoli, cut into small pieces
- ½ cup (65g) GF breadcrumbs, seasoned
- ½ cup (50g) grated tasty cheese
- 3 free range egg yolks (or 2 whole eggs if baby is over 1)

Preheat oven to 180°C. Line a baking tray with baking paper. Mix all ingredients together in a large bowl and form into nugget-like shapes. Pop onto baking tray and bake for 25 minutes, turning after 15. Serve warm.

Caramel Milk

- 2 cups (500ml) milk
- 5 tbs. (50g) brown sugar
- ¼ tsp. vanilla essence

Heat milk in a saucepan over medium heat. Stir in sugar and vanilla and serve warm.

Cheesy Frittata

- 1 large potato, peeled, thinly sliced and boiled until soft
- 3 free range eggs
- 50g cheddar cheese, grated
- 1 tbs. (15g) butter

Heat butter in a non-stick frying pan over medium heat, add potatoes. Whisk eggs and pour over potatoes, add cheese and cook until bubbles begin to appear on the surface. Flip when golden and cook underside. Cut into little soldiers to serve.

Creamy Rice

- 2 cups (370g) short grain rice
- 2 cups (500ml) milk
- 1 tsp. nutmeg

Bring 2 cups (500ml) water to boil. Add rice and cook until water is absorbed. Add milk and return to boil, then reduce heat and allow to simmer, stirring regularly. Cook for 15 minutes or until rice is tender. Allow to cool and serve sprinkled with nutmeg.

French Toast

- 1 egg
- 1 tbs. (15ml) milk
- 2 slices GF bread, crusts removed
- 1 tsp. butter

Beat egg with milk until well blended. Pour into a shallow dish. Cut each slice of bread into thirds. Heat butter in a non-stick frying pan. Dip bread into egg mixture, coating well both sides. Place coated bread into the frying pan and cook on both sides until golden brown. Serve with a drizzle of jam or honey.

Hint: This is a great way to use stale bread!

Pureed Apple & Cinnamon

- 1 apple, peeled and chopped
- ½ tsp. cinnamon sugar

Place apple in a saucepan and cover with water. Bring to the boil and allow to simmer until soft. Remove any excess liquid, add cinnamon and mash.

Sweet Potato Fries

- 1 sweet potato, peel and cut into small chips
- 2 tbs. olive oil
- 1 tsp. cinnamon sugar

Preheat oven 180°C. In a bag place potato chips and oil and shake until potatoes are coated. Pop onto a paper lined baking tray and sprinkle with cinnamon sugar. Turn to coat all sides then bake for 20–30 minutes, depending on the thickness of your chips, or until tender. Serve warm.

Tofu Nuggets

- 1 pkt firm tofu
- 1 free range egg yolk, beaten
- ¼ cup (40g) GF plain flour
- 1 tsp. garlic powder

Preheat oven to 180°C. Slice tofu into cubes or fingers manageable for your baby or toddler. Roll in egg yolk, coating well. Then into flour which has been seasoned with garlic powder and a little pepper. Chill in fridge for 5 minutes before baking for 15 minutes.

Optional: Add some GF breadcrumbs to the seasoning for a little crunch.

Note: Frozen bread grates more easily.

Vegie Fruit Mash

Flynn Turnbull's favourite.

- *1 green apple, peeled and chopped*
- *200g sweet potato, peeled and chopped*
- *Kernels from a corn on the cob*
- *6 plump blueberries*

Place apple, sweet potato and corn in a saucepan with 1½ cups water and boil until tender. Add blueberries and puree, serve warm.

If your baby is 'Beautiful and perfect, never cries or fusses, sleeps on schedule or burps on demand, an angel all the time' …
YOU'RE THE GRANDMA!

God Bless Grandmas

Drinks

It usually takes a long time to find a shorter way.

Anonymous

Apple Citrus Refresher

SERVES 4

- *2 granny smith apples, cored and chopped*
- *2 oranges, peeled and cut*
- *1 small lime, juiced*
- *2 cups (500ml) ginger ale*

Juice apple and orange. Pour juice into serving jug, add lime juice, mix and refrigerate. Just before serving, stir in ginger ale and serve in tall glasses over stacks of crushed ice.

Banana Fruit Frappe

SERVES 3

- *1 cup pineapple juice*
- *3 sliced bananas*
- *1 tbs. honey*
- *2 cups ice*

Combine all ingredients in a blender and puree until smooth.

Berry Blast

SERVES 2. Recipe by Sue Edmondstone.

- *100g frozen strawberries (can use fresh chilled strawberries as well)*
- *50g blueberries*
- *2 guavas, peeled*
- *2 freshly squeezed oranges*

Combine all ingredients in a blender and puree till smooth. Serve immediately.

Energiser Drink

SERVES 2

- *2 carrots, peeled*
- *1 cm piece of fresh ginger, peeled*
- *2 celery stalks*
- *2 oranges, peeled and chopped*

Place all ingredients in a juicer. Serve over crushed ice.

Jingo Juice

SERVES 4. A recipe by Marie McColl.

- *2 oranges*
- *3 tbs. blackcurrant syrup*
- *1.25 ltr. ginger ale*

Juice 1 ½ oranges and cut the other into thin wedges. Blend together orange juice, syrup, ginger ale and several ice cubes. Serve with remaining orange wedges.

Pink Slushies

SERVES 2. A recipe from Georgia Darr and Maddie Willson.

- *4 cups cubed watermelon*
- *3 tbs. lime juice*
- *⅔ cup (160ml) orange juice*
- *4 tbs. sugar*

In a blender, combine all ingredients. Fill with ice and blend until smooth. Pour into 4 tall glasses and serve.

Strawberry Lemonade

SERVES 4.

- *1 cup (220g) sugar*
- *4 lemons*
- *200g ripe strawberries, hulled and quartered*

Stir sugar and 2 cups water over low heat until sugar dissolves. Simmer 5 minutes. Add a further 3 cups water and juice and rind of lemons. Pour into a large jug. Add strawberries and chill. Serve over lots of crushed ice.

Tor's Piña Colada

SERVES 4. A Samoan staple!

- *1 small can crushed pineapple*
- *400ml can coconut cream*
- *1 cup (250ml) milk*

Place all ingredients into a large jug and blitz to blend. Stir and serve over crushed ice.

Tropical Delight

SERVES 2. Recipe by Majella Coleman.

- *1 cup of fresh pineapple, cubed*
- *1 banana*
- *250g passionfruit yoghurt*
- *2 tbs. honey*

Blend all ingredients together till smooth and serve with a few cubes of ice.

Virgin Mary

MAKES 1

- *1 cup (250ml) tomato juice*
- *1 tbs. lemon juice*
- *1 tsp. GF Worcestershire sauce*
- *4 drops Tabasco sauce*

Mix all ingredients in a jug and pour into a tall glass with crushed ice. Serve garnished with a trimmed stalk of fresh celery.

Herbs to the Rescue

The greatest sweetener of human life is friendship.

Unknown Author

Whether you are cooking a meal with just 4 or 40 ingredients you want it to be flavoursome! If you are taking the time the cook, you want it to be edible!!!

What we have found in cooking with just 4 or fewer ingredients is that it is imperative one of those ingredients has a strong, dramatic flavour. Often in a dip or a soup or a main dish in fact in many things this can be achieved by adding a fresh herb.

Here is a list of the herbs we have found most useful to us and what they complement, we hope you find it useful to!!!

Basil: *Basil is a perfect complement for tomatoes and features heavily in Italian cuisine. It also works beautifully with cheese, pasta, eggs, meat and salads, soups, pesto and casseroles. It is best torn, not cut and added to dishes just before serving as cooking diminishes its flavour.*

Chives: *Also known as green onions or scallions are the baby of the onion family. Chives add a great boost to the flavour of salads, potatoes, soups, sandwiches, dips, dressings and mayonnaise and are best added just before serving. Use chives to rub on meat or seafood before grilling.*

Coriander: *Or if you live in some parts of the world, Cilantro, is a fabulous accompaniment to most things Asian especially Thai and Indian. It has a particular affinity with chicken, fish, curries, stir-fries, chutneys and salads.*

Dill: *Did you know ... Dill leaves are used as a herb, but the actual seeds can be collected, dried and ground up as a spice? Dill works well with seafood, chicken, beetroot, cucumber, many vegetable dishes, eggs and vinegar.*

Mint: *If you haven't got a herb garden, start with mint as it is the most difficult of all herbs to kill! It has a fresh, crisp flavour and is fabulous in salads, or with seafood, lamb, peas, potatoes, yoghurt, fresh berries, fresh pineapple or break off a twig and pop it into a fruit punch or jug of water with ice. Use it to garnish desserts, especially chocolate ones.*

Oregano: Also known as wild majoram, is widely used in Italian cooking and is perfect in pastas and sprinkled on pizzas. Additionally it complements pork, chicken, aubergine, pepper, olives, courgette and sauces.

Parsley: Is the world's most popular herb! Like most fresh herbs it is high in vitamins and minerals and adds a delicious flavour to garlic, eggs, vegetables, cheese and potato dishes, fish, soups and poultry. Use it as garnish and sprinkled over salads and pizzas just before serving adds a healthy, fresh taste.

Tarragon: Adds a unique zing to seafood, chicken, lamb, tomato and sauces! Did you know: Béarnaise sauce is just Hollandaise with Tarragon (see Sauces).

Thyme: Is one of our personal favourites (apart from wishing we had more of it!!!) it is absolutely spectacular in our baked thyme and ricotta pie and our sautéed cherry tomatoes. It imparts a fabulous flavour to all kinds of red meat dishes, soups, sauces and vegetable dishes. It also provides a tasty stuffing for chicken.

Oils Explained

I stand in front of the oil aisle at my local supermarket with literally hundreds of bottles looking back at me and I wonder to myself ... What is the difference????

Confused Shopper

These are the oils we have used within the pages of *4 Ingredients Gluten Free*. Our research and questions unearthed the following information.

Virgin and Regular Olive Oil: Olive oil comes in varying grades from extra virgin to a blended mix found in most supermarkets. To explain the difference it is interesting to note how oil is produced.

1st step. Olives are picked, sorted and washed

2nd step. They are placed in a press to extract the oil, this is known as the first or 'virgin' press and gives rise to what we call Extra Virgin Oil. When buying look for the words 'first, cold pressed' on the label to ensure you are buying the correct oil. This oil is THE best to buy as it hasn't been heated and therefore still loaded in flavour and nutrients. It is best used in salads or at the very end of a cooking process.

3rd step. A second press produces Virgin Oil. During this process the oil is slightly heated thereby losing some of its nutrients and flavour. Virgin Oil is best used in most types of cooking except for frying as its ignition point (the point where it will catch alight) is relatively low.

4th step. The third press process produces Olive Oil, this oil is best used in all general cooking.

Avocado Oil: This oil is made from pressing the flesh of avocados. It compliments seafood and salads and can be drizzled over roasts prior to baking. It is sensational in the place of peanut or sesame oil in salads

Grapeseed Oil: is a vegetable oil pressed from the seeds of various varieties of Vitis vinifera grapes, an abundant by-product of winemaking. This oil is fabulous in salad dressings and also in barbecue marinades as it has a very unobtrusive flavour.

Macadamia oil: Macadamia oil is cold-pressed from the nuts of the macadamia tree. Macadamia oil is the 'creme de la creme' of nut oils. It is an excellent frying oil due to its high ignition point and LOADED in nutrients.

Sunflower Oil: Is ideal for use as a general cooking oil and, because of its very mild taste, at those time when you don't want a strong intrusive flavour such as in making mayonnaise and baking cakes and frying.

Sesame Oil: This naturally is obtained from sesame seeds. It is a very flavoursome oil and should be used sparingly as a dressing for salads and in stir-fries. It is best to use only a small amount due to its low ignition point to ensure the oil doesn't smoke.

Walnut Oil: With a delicate, nutty flavour, this oil is perfect in a salad dressing, drizzled over steamed vegetables, flavouring for fish or steak or for use in baking.

Handy Home Tips

Dream … Believe … Create … Succeed

Rachael Bermingham

Aching feet and chesty colds: *Apply a thick coat of chest rub and cover feet with a pair of socks before going to bed at night.*

Baby oil removes crayon: *No need to buy expensive cleaners to remove unwanted crayon artwork from walls — all you need is baby oil! Red crayon may be a little more stubborn, but one wipe is usually all it takes!*

Baby wipes: *Are great for brightening kids' white leather shoes.*

Basil oil: *To make basil oil soak some excess basil leaves in a jar of olive oil. Yummy drizzled over salads or used in frying meats, cheeses etc.*

Bathroom odours: *Place an opened box of baking soda or an open container of activated charcoal behind the toilet to absorb bathroom odours.*

Broken glass: *Pick up small shards of glass that remain after clearing the big pieces by blotting the area with wet newspapers. The tiny fragments will stick to the paper.*

Bubblegum in hair: *To remove, simply rub some peanut butter onto the gummed hair. You will need to wash the hair afterwards but it helps the gum slide off the hair.*

Butter: *For softened butter in a hurry, grate it — it works a treat.*

Cake tins: *Use dry cake mixture to line a cake tin, rather than flour to have no 'flour' look on the outside of the cake.*

Candle holders: *To prevent the wax from melting and sticking to the inside of a votive candle holder, pour a bit of water in the holder, then place the candle on top. If you're reading this tip too late, and there's already wax stuck inside your candle holder, pop it in the freezer for an hour. The wax will chip right off.*

Candle wax: *To remove wax from carpeting or other fabric, first scrape away any excess. Then place a brown paper bag over the wax and run a warm iron over the bag. The wax will melt right into the bag! Continue moving the bag around as you pick up the wax so you are always using a clean section. If a little grease stain remains on carpet, sprinkle with baking soda and allow to sit overnight before vacuuming, which will remove the grease residue. If coloured wax leaves a stain on carpet, blot with spot remover or carpet cleaner, following label directions.*

CDs: *Repair scratched CDs by rubbing over smooth peanut butter and wiping off with a coffee filter.*

Clothes pegs: *Use a clip on clothes peg to hold nails in place when hammering in hard-to-reach places.*

Coffee & tea stains: *Remove coffee and tea stains from rugs by pouring a little beer over the stain. Lightly rub the beer into the material, and the stain should disappear. You may have to do it a couple of times to remove all stains.*

Coffee filter: *A coffee filter is microwave safe, and makes a great cover over food to prevent splattering when cooking in the microwave.*

Coffee mugs: *Clean coffee stained mugs by rinsing out, then rubbing in salt. Leave for approx. 5 minutes before rinsing. Stains should be removed. You may have to repeat.*

Cold press: *Keep a cold press on hand, by rinsing a face washer in cold water, and whilst still wet place in a snap lock bag and freeze. Next time you need a cold press just wrap in a tea towel and apply.*

Computer keyboards: *Clean computer keyboards with nail-polish remover and an old toothbrush. Simply moisten the brush with remover and lightly rub the keys.*

Cookbook: *Keep cookbooks clean from splatters when cooking by placing in a clear plastic bag.*

Crayon on walls or washable wallpaper: Spray with WD-40®, then gently wipe, using a paper towel or clean cloth. If the mark is stubborn, sprinkle a little baking soda on a damp sponge and gently rub in a circular motion. If the WD-40® leaves a residue, gently wipe off with a sponge soaked in soapy water; rinse clean; blot dry. Another method is to use a hair dryer — it heats the wax and wipes away instantly. If the color remains, like red usually does, wet a cloth with bleach and wipe.

Dryer tip: Include a few tennis balls in each dryer cycle. The tennis balls not only cut drying time by 25% — 50%, but also fluff the clothes to a delicate softness, and towels will be especially fluffy.

Dusting and polishing: Oven mitts are great for dusting and polishing furniture. Use one side of the mitt to apply wax or polish to your furniture and the other side to buff it up. Wash afterwards to use again and again.

Fatigue: Take a glass of grapefruit and lemon juice in equal parts to dispel fatigue and general tiredness after a day's work.

Fresh flowers: To keep cut flowers from sagging in their vase, crisscross several piece of transparent tape across the mouth of the vase, leaving space where you can insert the flowers. The flowers will look perky and fresh for a few extra days.

Hair dye: Run a bit of Vaseline across your hairline to stop hair dye staining your skin if it seeps off.

Hair conditioner: Use to protect your shoes during winter. Lather your shoes or boots with conditioner. It is also a good leather conditioner.

Hangover: Eat honey on GF crackers. The fructose in the honey will help to flush out the alcohol in your system.

Headache: Eat 10–12 almonds, the equivalent of two aspirins, for a migraine headache. Almonds are far less likely to upset the stomach.

Ink stains: Remove ink stains by rubbing alcohol on the stain before washing.

Insect bites: Mix water with cornstarch into a paste and apply. This is effective in drawing out the poisons of most insect bites and is also an effective remedy for nappy rash. Calendula oil also works brilliantly.

Ironing: Add a drop of your favourite essential oil to the water in your iron to give your clothes a lovely fragrance. And if ironing delicates, no need to adjust heat settings just cover with baking paper and iron.

Jewellery: Give jewellery a great sparkle by placing in a glass of warm water and dropping in an Alka-Seltzer tablet for a couple of minutes. Polish with a soft cloth.

Kids' artwork: If your want to save some your kids' precious artwork, simply roll up the artwork and place inside a paper-towel tube. Label the outside with the child's name and date.

Kitty litter: To keep cat litter fresh smelling, mix baby powder in with the litter.

Lipstick stains: Get rid of lipstick stains from cloth napkins by dabbing with Vaseline before popping in the washing machine.

Microwave cleaning: Food splatters all over the inside of your microwave and cooks itself on after time. To easily remove this mess, place a sponge soaked in water in the microwave. Cook on high heat for 2 minutes, then allow it to sit without opening the microwave door for 5 minutes. The filth is now ready to be wiped right off — no scrubbing — and your sponge is right there!

Milk cartons: Slice the top off a 2 or 3 litre milk bottle. Fill with food scraps for the compost heap.

Mosquito bites: Apply lime juice diluted with water on bites with a cotton ball.

Mothball substitute: Take your leftover soap slivers and put them in a vented plastic bag. Place the bag with seasonal clothes before packing them away. Not only will the scent prevent them from moth harm, but also they'll smell great when you pull them out.

Nail polish: Keep nail polish fresh and easy to use by storing in the refrigerator.

Odd socks: Save on purchasing sponges for your car. Slip an odd sock over your hand and use as a cleaning mitt with your normal car wash detergent.

Oil stains on concrete: *Remove unsightly grease, oil and transmission fluid stains off your concrete driveway or garage floor by spraying with oven cleaner. Let settle for 5–10 mins, then scrub with a stiff brush and rinse.*

Paint brushes: *When taking a break from painting, wrap brushes in cling film. They will stay moist and wet for a couple of hours.*

Pillowcases: *Use pillow cases to keep linen sets together. Use one pillow case and fold up and place inside both sheets and the other pillow case. No more searching for matching pieces.*

Popcorn: *Eliminate unpopped popcorn duds by keeping your unpopped supply in the freezer.*

Potatoes: *Stop potatoes from budding by storing an apple with them.*

Red wine: *Remove red wine stains from carpet. While the stain is still wet pour on some white wine to dilute the colour, then clean with a sponge and cold water. Sprinkle the area with salt and wait 10 minutes before vacuuming up the mess.*

Repel insects: *Dilute 1tbs. of vanilla extract into 1 cup of water and wipe the mixture on any exposed skin to discourage mosquitoes, bush flies and ticks.*

Scissors: *To sharpen old scissors use them to cut up a sheet of aluminium foil. The more you cut, the sharper the scissors become.*

Shaving cuts: *Dab a bit of lip balm directly onto the nick and the bleeding from most shaving cuts will quickly stop.*

Smelly feet: *Soak feet in strong tea for 20 minutes every day until the smell disappears. To prepare your footbath, brew two tea bags in 2½ cups of water for 15 minutes and pour the tea into a basin containing two litres of cool water.*

Sore throat: *Mix 1 tsp. lime juice and 1 tbs. honey. Swallow tiny amounts slowly 2–3 times a day.*

Speed-dry nail polish: *Spray painted nails with a coat of olive-oil cooking spray and let it dry; the spray is also a great moisturiser for your hands.*

Spilt eggs: *Clean up spilled uncooked egg by sprinkling with salt. It will draw the egg together and you can easily wipe it up with a sponge or paper towel.*

Splinters: *Lay scotch tape over the splinter and pull off or soak the area in vegetable oil for a few minutes before removing with tweezers.*

Stain removers: *Reach for baby wipes anytime you notice something on yours or the kids' clothes — sees it gone in no time. We don't know what is in them, but they work a treat.*

Stickers, decals, and glue: *To remove them from furniture, glass, plastic, etc. saturate with vegetable oil and rub off.*

White-Out / Liquid Paper and permanent marker stains: *Dab some sunscreen over the stain and rub off with a paper towel. Repeat until stain is gone.*

Zippers: *To make a zipper slide up and down more smoothly, rub a bar of soap over the teeth.*

Biographies

Rachael Bermingham

Rachael Bermingham (nee Moore) was born in Stanthorpe on the Darling Downs before moving to the Sunshine Coast in primary school.

A born commerce entrepreneur Rachael opened her first business, a hair salon, at age 19 before selling it for a profit and moving into other exciting careers including diving, shark feeding and travel.

Rachael's talent and passion for growing multi million dollar businesses from home through her clever marketing, publicity, time management and goal strategies soon developed into a full time consulting and mentoring business with women clients in six different countries.

Soon Rachael was being asked to talk on marketing, business building and life balance and her reputation as an inspirational keynote speaker blossomed.

Upon the birth of her first son, Jaxson, Rachael's desire to be a full time Mum led her to transform the contents of her talks into her first co-written and self published book to inspire women to achieve their goals called *Read My Lips* — this was to become her first bestselling book and would be the catalyst for her lifelong family friend Kim to confide in her about her own idea for a book — a cookbook with only a few ingredients.

Rachael's experience in self publishing, marketing, and her enthusiasm to have such a book herself merged with Kim's fabulous idea to produce all the winning ingredients the girls needed to co write Rachael's second and most famous bestseller to date called *4 Ingredients*.

A devoted and energetic mum, Rachael has since written four books around her proudest role of being a mum — all of which are bestsellers and are all self published, self marketed and self funded. *Read My Lips* is a motivational book for women Rachael co-wrote while breastfeeding her son Jaxson, *4 Ingredients* was co-written with Kim during Jaxson's day sleeps, *4 Ingredients 2* co-written during his night sleeps and her latest bestseller prompted by thousands of emails on how to write and market your own book — *How to write your own book & make it a bestseller* — was solo written.

Having just returned from the UK with Kim after successfully launching *4 Ingredients* in Britain and Ireland, Rachael is excited about her and Kim's television series, *4 Ingredients*, which first premiered on The LifeStyle Channel in September 2008. The series is incredibly popular and the girls received a nomination for Favourite Female Personality at the 2009 ASTRA Awards.

Fun-loving and a real go getter, Rachael lives on the Sunshine Coast in Queensland. When she's not working on new books, having fun speaking on stage or cooking up a terrific *4 Ingredient* storm with Kim, Rachael can be found enjoying what she loves most — chillaxing on her acreage property with her wonderful husband of 13 years, Paul, (a house renovator), her gorgeous son Jaxson who is now 4, step-daughters Lee, 20, and Teri, 18, and their fabulous friends enjoying the spectacular sun, surf and sand of the Sunshine Coast.

Happy Cooking!

You can contact Rachael by email: **Rachael@4ingredients.com.au**

Or by snail mail: **PO Box 1171 Mooloolaba QLD 4557.**

Rachael's other business website links:

Speaking information, bookings, and information about Rachael's other books can be found at **www.RachaelBermingham.com**

Kim McCosker

Kim was born in Stanthorpe and raised there until moving to Mundubbera, Queensland, a fantastic little town where many of her wonderful family and friends still live.

Schooled on the Gold Coast, Kim attended Star of the Sea Catholic High School and Griffith University, completing a degree in International Finance in 1998. Kim trained with MLC as a Financial Planner completing her Diploma in Financial Planning through Deakin University in 2000. Kim's natural ease with people, her ability to communicate effortlessly and her home grown, country confidence served her extremely well as a successful financial adviser and later as the Queensland State Manager of MLC Private Client Services. After the birth of her second child Kim resigned and decided to contract from home writing financial plans.

It was during this phase of her life that 4 Ingredients was turned into reality. Kim had the idea, but it was at the insistence of her life long friend Rachael Bermingham that they write the book ... And so over a couple of red wines began the *wonderful* rollercoaster ride *4 Ingredients* would go on to become!

Taking a year to compile and cook, *4 Ingredients* (or Kim's fourth child as she lovingly refers to it) was launched on the 14th March, 2007. From an initial print run of 2,000 that was deemed 'Over ambitious in a market *saturated* with cookbooks' Kim and Rachael went on to orchestrate what the trade now refers to simply as '*An Absolute Phenomenon!*'. Not only was 4 ingredients one of the biggest selling titles in both Australia and New Zealand for 2007 but it was **THE BIGGEST SELLING BOOK in Australia for 2008!**

On the back of the *extraordinary success* of the book, Kim and Rachael have now filmed two TV series also titled '*4 Ingredients*' for the Lifestyle Channel. Have launched a very clever application in **iTunes** that allows you to download the *4 Ingredients* app through iTunes onto your iPod Touch or iPhone. Are about to launch their own cookware range in all major department stores across Australia, which they can't wait to stock in their own kitchens, and have just returned from an extremely successful book launch into the UK and Irish markets.

And as Kim says "No-one is more surprised than us!!!!"

In addition to this, over the past 8 years Glen and Kim have bought and renovated several properties, including a beautiful 1957 Anglican Church, a beachside shack, and the current property they now live in on the Sunshine Coast's glorious Pelican Waters. Kim maintains the administration, bookwork and finances for their various business and financial interests.

Without a sliver of doubt however, the *most rewarding* of everything accomplished to date has been the birth of her three precious little boys Morgan, 7 Hamilton 4 and Flynn, 1. For Kim, family is *THE MOST IMPORTANT* thing in the world and carries the greatest priority of all she does! Renovations to properties were done with the children playing in the yard, recipes tested with them mixing and stirring, books written around their sleep times and trips made only when her wonderfully supportive and very loved husband Glen could be home for them.

Life presents many opportunities, but having the courage and the time to pursue them, in what is an ever increasingly busy and demanding world, is hard. But Kim is living proof that you can achieve whatever you want in life with exactly that ... *HARD WORK.*

Be Fabulous
Be You!

You can contact Kim through:
www.4ingredients.co.uk or
kim@4ingredients.com.au

Letter from a Parent

My son Joel has Aspergers, he has been on a gluten free diet for 4 years now.

This book is a godsend!!!

Finding gluten free recipes is challenging for parents like me, especially ones with only 4 Ingredients that are also cost effective!!

A gluten free diet has improved Joel's concentration ten fold. He is no longer in a lost world of his own and can even make eye contact with us now and that makes this Mum's heart sing!

I thoroughly recommend this diet and 4 Ingredients Gluten Free to everyone, especially parents of children with ASD, ADHD, ADD and the like.

Thanks Rachael & Kim, this has made life so much easier!

Susan Shillig.
Currimundi, Queensland, Australia.

Bibliography

Books

Cyndi O'Meara. **Changing Habits Changing Lives**. Penguin Books Victoria Australia, 2000.

Cyndi O'Meara. **Changing Habits Changing Lives Cookbook**. Penguin Books Victoria Australia, 2002.

Magazine of the Coeliac Society of Australia December 2008 edition. The Australian Coeliac Society, Waitara, NSW.

Take 5 Top Tips. ACP Magazines a division of ACP PBL Media Pty Ltd. ACP AMgazines LTD, 2009.

Danna Korn. **Living Gluten-Free for Dummies**. Wiley Publishing, Inc. 111 River St, Hoboken, NJ 07030-5774, 2006.

Anne Hillis & Penelope Stone. **Breast Bottle Bowl**. Harper Collins Publishers, 25 Ryde Road, Pymble, Sydney NSW 2073, 1993.

Tortilla International. Cole Group, Inc. 1330 N. Dutton Avenue., Suite 103 Santa Roase, CA 95410, 1995.

Oneka Lai. **Popular Rice Dishes**. Australian Universities Press, 169 Phillip street, Waterloo, NSW, 1973.

Nell Heaton. **Cookery To-day and To-morrow**. The Syndicate Publishing Co Ltd, 52 Long Acre WC2, 1946.

Richard J. Coppedge Jr., C.M.B. **Gluten Free Baking with The Culinary Institue of America**. Adams Media, 57 Littlefield Street, Avon, MA 02322. USA, 2008.

Joanna Whitby. **Practical Cooking for Babies and Toddlers**. Choice Books 57 Carrington Road, Marrickville NSW 2204, 1999.

For a free monthly 4 ingredient recipe subscribe at www.4ingredients.co.uk

Bibliography

Webpages

What is Coeliac Disease?
www.coeliacsociety.com.au/
www.coeliacresearchfund.org

Gluten Free Diets
www.gastro.net.au/diets/glutenfree.html

Gluten Free and Easy
www.glutenfreeandeasy.com/Active/ingredients.html

Coeliac Resources
www.basco.com.au/

Recipes and Tips
www.basicingredients.com.au/GF.html

Gluten Free Foods
www.glutenfreedirect.com.au/
www.glutenfreegoodies.com.au

How To Pack a Healthy Gluten-Free School Lunch for Your Gluten-Free Child
http://glutenfreecooking.about.com/od/glutenfreekids/ht/gflunchboxtips.htm

Gluten Free Gobsmacked
http://glutenfree.wordpress.com/2008/08/21/gluten-free-lunch-to-go-ideas-for-what-to-pack/

All I Really Need To Know I Learned in Kindergarten
www.robertfulghum.com/

For a free monthly 4 ingredient recipe subscribe at www.4ingredients.co.uk

Bibliography

Finger food ideas for making homemade baby food.

www.wholesomebabyfood.com/content/babyfoodFingerFoods.pdf

Herbs Explained by Jenelle Johnson

www.iolaregister.com/Local%20News/Stories/Herbsexplained.html

Herbs and Spices

www.gourmetgarden.com/au/

The essential guide to oils

http://recipefinder.ninemsn.com.au/article.aspx?id=281737

For a free monthly 4 ingredient recipe subscribe at www.4ingredients.co.uk

Index of Contents

Invitation

Join our online cooking school

To all who have contributed a recipe in this book by way of email, mail or phone we would like to extend our sincerest THANKS, your suggestions have been invaluable.

If YOU have a 4 Ingredient recipe and think others would enjoy cooking it, please visit us on our FACEBOOK page, we'd LOVE to meet you! Join us for our weekly on-line cooking school where you will see us making some of our fabulous 4 Ingredient recipes - you will be super surprised just how easy it is! We also share our hints on how to save time and money in the kitchen and you even have the chance to win some great prizes!

Visit us at www.facebook.com/4ingredients

Thank You

Best Wishes & Happy Cooking!

Rachael & Kim

www.4ingredients.co.uk

Ingredients

GLUTEN FREE